Covered Wagon Days

The Sun Dance of the Shoshones

Covered Wagon Days

A journey across the plains in the sixties,
and pioneer days in the Northwest;
from the private journals of
Albert Jerome Dickson

edited by
ARTHUR JEROME DICKSON

Introduction by A. B. Guthrie, Jr.

University of Nebraska Press
Lincoln and London

Introduction copyright © 1989 by the University of Nebraska
Press
Copyright 1929 by the Arthur H. Clark Company
Renewal copyright © 1957 by the Arthur H. Clark Company
All rights reserved
Manufactured in the United States of America

First Bison Book printing: 1989
Most recent printing indicated by the last digit below:
10   9   8   7   6   5   4   3   2

Library of Congress Cataloging-in-Publication Data
Dickson, Albert Jerome, b. 1849 or 50.
    Covered wagon days: a journey across the plains in the sixties
and pioneer days in the Northwest / from the private journals of
Albert Jerome Dickson: edited by Arthur Jerome Dickson: introduction by A. B. Guthrie, Jr.
      p.   cm.
    Reprint. Originally published: Cleveland: A. H. Clark, 1929.
Includes index.
    ISBN 0-8032-6582-4 (alk. paper)
    1. West (U.S.)—Description and travel—1860–1880. 2. Over-
land journeys to the Pacific. 3. Dickson, Albert Jerome, b. 1849
or 50—Diaries. 4. Pioneers—West (U.S.)—Diaries. 5. Frontier
and pioneer life—Northwest, Pacific. I. Dickson, Arthur Jerome. II. Title.
F594.D55   1989
917.804'2—dc 20   89-4934 CIP

Reprinted by arrangement with the Arthur H. Clark Company

To

MY FATHER, Albert Jerome Dickson, and the men
and women of an earlier day, whose courage
and vision have made possible the development
of the Northwest into a free and prosperous region, I dedicate this volume.

ARTHUR JEROME DICKSON

Contents

Illustrations

8 ILLUSTRATIONS

---

[1]Reproduced by courtesy of State Highway Department of Wyoming.
[2]Reproduced by courtesy of Mrs. A. C. Stohr.
[3]Reproduced by courtesy of C. W. Rank.
[4]Reproduced by courtesy of Great Northern Railway.

Introduction to the Bison Book Edition
By A. B. Guthrie, Jr.

This book came as an astonishment to me. I had read and studied many nonfiction works about America's westering and knew a good deal about Montana gold camps and early agriculture in the Gallatin Valley. But never had I read or even heard about Arthur Jerome Dickson's *Covered Wagon Days,* though it was copyrighted in 1929. I have filled that gap now and am happy that I have.

In the spring of 1864 Albert Jerome Dickson, father of the author, left La Crosse, Wisconsin, bound for the goldfields of Montana. He was a mere fourteen years old, a member of the household of Joshua and Rebecca Ridgley, themselves a part of a wagon train, drawn by oxen, that numbered only three wagons at the outset.

Throughout the trip and on his eventual return by way of the Missouri River, the boy kept copious notes. It was from them that his son put together this narrative, in which the father speaks in the first person.

The result is a detailed and constantly interesting story. It is as if the young boy, infinitely curious himself, were intent on transferring his experiences and observations to others. Where else to find out how to build a wagon or train an ox to the yoke?

He describes the dress of his companions, their physical appearance, their concern about and preparations against Indian attacks, the look of the changing land, the feel of cool water, the slow, slow pace of the oxen.

The party, joined later by others and sometimes lessened by departures, made its way to Omaha and shortly was on the trail up the Platte River valley, over the now well-rutted Oregon Trail.

The boy was driving the second wagon of the Ridgley outfit and otherwise doing a man's work, though once he was pulled off night duty in Indian country because he was deemed too young. He had time, or found it somehow, to record their day-by-days, the weather, the difficulties with river crossings, the sight of buffalo and elk, the meals that Mrs. Ridgley, a brave and industrious little woman, contrived. Nothing seems to have escaped him. Later, if in doubt about something or ignorant of it, he sought out characters who knew.

The train kept to the trail, passing Courthouse and Chimney Rocks and the Sweetwater gap, where the river boiled through a cleft in the mountains. The newly traveled Bozeman Trail, which veered off through the heart of Indian country, they rejected as too dangerous. They also passed up the Bridger Road, a somewhat less dangerous route to the west of the Bridger Trail. It was from Idaho that they ventured up into the gold camps of the newly established territory of Montana, to Bannock and Virginia City.

But mining and gold camps were not for the Ridgleys and some of the others. They moved north to the rich fields of the Gallatin Valley, where they farmed. Almost the only source of outside information in the valley was the *Montana Post*, published at Virginia City. Dickson gives some quotations from it, including one that must have tickled him. It was: "A clergyman at an afternoon service was asked to read a notice for a women's rights meeting, which he did in this wise, 'At half past six o'clock in the school house, in the first district, a hen will attempt to crow.' "

He was alive to everything that touched him. In his notes he found time to give a sketchy but accurate account of vigilante days in Montana and the hanging of Sheriff Henry Plummer, leader of the outlaws.

After a few years in Gallatin Valley, Dickson decided to return east, going by way of the Missouri River. As he says in his conclusion, "I had driven an ox-team across the Plains 1700 miles to Gallatin valley, returned by boat down the Missouri 2100 miles, with a good 600 miles more across country with horses to complete the circle—in all about 4500 miles."

And he was still a very young man. Perhaps that is what makes his book so interesting—his youth and youthful curiosity and the uncomplaining hardihood of the green years.

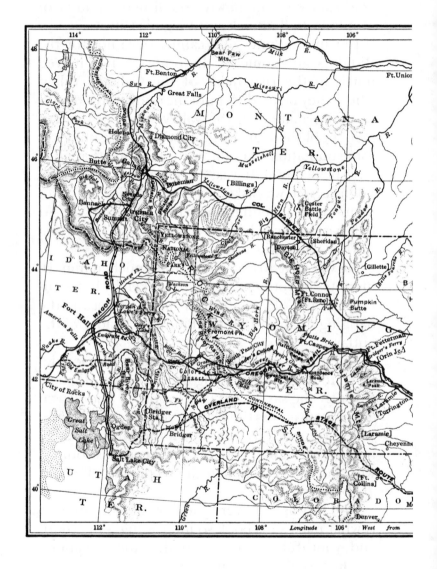

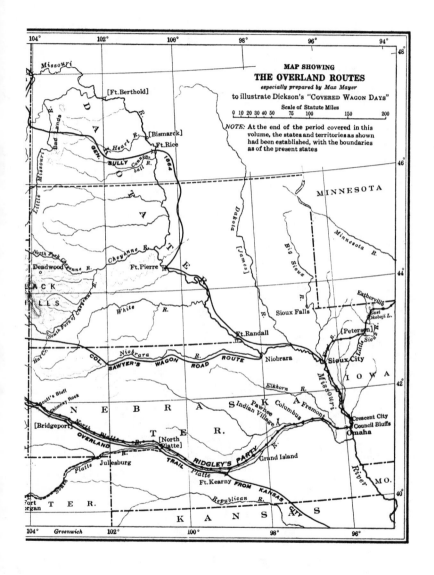

MAP SHOWING
THE OVERLAND ROUTES
especially prepared by Max Mayer
to illustrate Dickson's "Covered Wagon Days"

Scale of Statute Miles
0 10 20 30 40 50   75   100   150   200

NOTE: At the end of the period covered in this
volume, the states and territories as shown
had been established, with the boundaries
as of the present states

Preface

This work is a portrayal of pioneer life in the Northwest, with the intimate details of everyday living presented in their historical setting. It was begun in the belief that a simple narrative of events dealing with that stirring period would carry its own appeal. The romance of the West will never be written until the lives of the men and women who figured then are seen in their true perspective. Fortunately there are still a few living who can aid us in this, and the message they give us will help to keep alive the spirit of the old West, which is so vital to our welfare.

The present volume is an authentic narrative of the experiences of my father, Albert Jerome Dickson, in the sixties. My father, who is still living, kept a journal in which he recorded the everyday happenings in the life of a plainsman, including an account of a journey by covered-wagon "across," a description of life in the mining camps and adjacent settlements, and a return trip by boat down the Missouri river. It is a story of overland travel and the technic of the trail; of indian raids and border treaties; of pioneer organizations and the formation of territorial government; of the interplay of forces concerned with law and order, involving the activities of road agents and the Vigilantes; of men, like Bozeman and Bridger, who blazed the way westward.

In the preparation of this manuscript I have adhered strictly to the facts as presented in my father's original memoranda, notes, journals, and private papers. With my deep personal interest in the pioneer days of the West, I have read many of the narratives published, but I believe I can truthfully say that in the present volume is set down a more authentic account of real conditions than has so far been published.

Responsibility for any errors contained herein rests wholly with myself. Appreciation is due the following:

Dr. Grace Raymond Hebard for a critical reading of the text, for encouragement in the work and many helpful suggestions; my publisher, Arthur H. Clark, for his critical reading of the original manuscript and valuable suggestions in the extensive revision thereof; Mary Roberts Rinehart for valuable assistance in organizing the material; Wilber King for help in gathering data; David Hilger and his staff, of the Montana Historical Society, and Mrs. Cyrus Beard, of the Wyoming Historical Society, for access to source material and personal help; Rodolphe Petter, M. K. Sniffen, J. M. Hamilton, Ira H. Butterfield, and many others for friendly criticism and literary assistance.

ARTHUR JEROME DICKSON

Chapter I

The Covered Wagon Start from
La Crosse, Wisconsin

The Covered Wagon Start from La Crosse, Wisconsin

On the fifth of May, 1864, a little caravan of three covered wagons passed down the main street of La Crosse, Wisconsin, ferried across the Mississippi to the Minnesota side by the diagonal route past the head of Barron's island, and began its toilsome journey westward. The oxen, responding to the crack of whips and the sharp command of the drivers, struck the same plodding gait which has carried the vanguard of many a civilization across the leagues to the land of its desire. The wagon tilts of new canvas shone white against a background of early green. The roads were still heavy from recent rains, and there was a straining of gear and a rumble of wheels whenever a muddy place was encountered.

From the ferry landing and the lime-kiln near by, their way lay across marshy lowlands over roads that were graded and in places "corduroyed" to insure solid footing. A mile of this, and then a steep climb brought them to the first bench, where, overlooking the river bottom, the village of La Crescent lay half hidden among her oaks and elms.

The day, which had begun fair, was now little more than half spent when the sky became overcast and a storm seemed imminent. The wagons were thereupon driven to a spot sheltered from the rising wind, the oxen were outspanned, and preparations were made to camp for the night.

Gathered a little later around their first campfire were five venturesome souls who had cut loose from their moorings for the overland trip "across." Joshua Ridgley and his wife, Rebecca, belonged with the first wagon. For some years they had kept a tavern at their farm six miles above La Crosse on the West Salem road. Mr. Ridgley – or "Dad," as he was familiarly called – was a man in his later prime, full six feet tall and powerfully built. He wore a closely-cropped beard and clothing suitable for outdoor wear – flat-crowned felt hat, a blouse or "wampus," jeans trousers, and cowhide boots. Having trekked from Maryland, his native state, to Pennsylvania when he was a young man, and thence to Wisconsin fourteen years before this narrative begins, he was tacitly accepted as leader of the party.

Mrs. Ridgley was a sprightly little woman, very trim in her everyday dress of figured calico, fashioned with the short waist, plain sleeves, broad belt, and full skirt of the Civil war period. Besides being a notable cook and housekeeper, she was "good in sickness." It was also remembered that she could speak her mind on occasion.

Belonging in the Ridgley household was a well-grown lad in his fourteenth year, by name Jerome Dickson, who drove the second team and who ap-

JEROME DICKSON

pears in this narrative in the first person. His connection with the Ridgley family began three years earlier following the arrival of a stepfather in the home when, by mutual agreement and according to a current practice, he had been bound out to Mr. and Mrs. Ridgley until he should come of age. In return for his services he was to be allowed to attend the public school in winter and to receive, besides his "keep," a horse and saddle and other property amounting in all to five hundred dollars on the day that he was to be twenty-one. He is chiefly characterized by a fondness for adventuring in out-of-the-way places, preferably barefoot whenever weather conditions and the absence of sandburs and cactus permitted.

There remain Deacon Sylvester Smith and his son, Alonzo, of North La Crosse, who took turns with the third team. Deacon Smith was a roly-poly, gray-whiskered little man in his fifties, mild mannered and of an invariable good nature. Never but once have I known him to use profanity. But of that later. Since his wife's death he and his son had batched by themselves on their little truck farm. He was a deacon of the Baptist faith, and if ever a man lived his religion, Deacon Smith did.

Alonzo was a ruddy, wholesome fellow of seventeen or eighteen, with a passion for hunting and other outdoor activities. I think his greatest desire as well as mine was to get out West where there were indians to fight.

Gold had been discovered in the mountains of

southwestern Montana, then a part of Idaho territory. Reports had been current for over a year of its existence in paying quantities at Bannack, in Beaver Head valley. Then came accounts of still greater discoveries in Alder Gulch, where Virginia City had sprung up almost overnight and was the goal of many an overland party for months before the news had reached our section. The air was full of it by now. Which accounts for our presence here on our westward exodus.

The deacon and Alonzo had joined us that forenoon in La Crosse by previous arrangement. One of the Farnham brothers, local merchants, had been getting a couple of loads of goods ready to be used in starting a store at the mines and expected to go with us also. Greatly to our disappointment, however, he could not start until the following week, and we were forced to proceed without him. The two Philipps brothers, neighbors from up Salem way, had gone on ahead, expecting to complete their outfitting and fall in with us later.

Our enjoyment of the campfire was interrupted before long when the gathering storm sent us into our wagons. Here it was pleasant to lie and listen to the rain as it pattered upon the wagon cover, knowing that the canvas of heavy duck would turn water as effectually as our shingled roof at home.

Chapter II
Westward - Ho!

Westward - Ho!

We were up betimes next morning. By the time the cattle were fed and the milking done, breakfast was ready.

There is nothing that surpasses a meal cooked over a campfire. And it takes an appetite sharpened by life in the open to do it justice. The bacon and eggs, fried potatoes, salt-rising bread, and coffee of that first breakfast I shall never forget.

The weather was still unsettled and we decided to wait awhile before yoking up. This gave me an opportunity to slip over to the edge of the bluff for a parting look.

There before me was the river, silent and unhurried. Her waters were tinged with amber from the pines and fenlands of her upper reaches. Grove-clad islands of a haunting loveliness gave sanctuary to countless flocks of migrant wildfowl. On the hither shore the ferry was discharging a mixed load. I could make out wagons, horses and cattle-movers, probably bound for western Minnesota or Iowa, where land could be taken up under the newly-enacted homestead law. Beyond the river lay the two towns of North La Crosse and La Crosse proper, connected by the mile-long Plank road across the intervening marsh-land. Smoke from the mills and factories floated lazily over the valley. Grandad's Bluff rose on the east, and to the north, French island divided the current of Black river at its confluence with the Mississippi. Here were the squat wigwams of a Winnebago indian village. These indians were now literally swarming over the river in their fleet dugouts, spearing buffalo fish during the run. A clumsy grain barge from down river, towed by half a dozen tugs, was making for the landing. From far upstream the strains of a calliope came softly. I knew by this that presently a steamboat plying between Saint Paul and Saint Louis would halt briefly on her downward course. In every direction as far as the eye could reach lay virgin forests of hardwood – hickory, cherry, ash, walnut, and the different species of oak. Along the river bottom elm and cottonwood abounded.

As I looked, a shaft of sunlight, falling through a rift in the clouds, touched the river mists and gave them soft transition of color and light against the horizon. It was a picture to linger over, holding as it did all that life had brought me thus far. I could not have given my thoughts expression in words. Nor did the prospect of going west to fight indians wholly overcome the reluctance with which I finally made my way back to camp.

The sky was now gradually clearing and we made short work of our preparations for starting. The oxen yoked and in their places, the two milch cows tied behind the forward wagons, and the "grub boxes" in, we were ready to travel.

For some hours we followed the ridge northward, paralleling the river. Then we swung away from the bluffs, out upon a broad expanse of rolling prairie crossed by numerous streams whose course was marked by a thick growth of timber. The roads were muddy, but traveling was easier on the upland and we were loaded light.

We were three days on our way to Chatfield, the next town, through a region of open forests of hardwood on the higher ground and intervening meadows, vividly green and gay with early wild flowers. The air was alive with the song of birds and the chatter of squirrels. We passed numerous farmhouses substantially built of log or frame. Much of the land had been entered under the preemption act, by which title to a quarter section could be acquired after a six months' residence and a cash payment to the government of $1.25 per acre. Soldier's "scrip" when obtainable could also be applied on government land.

The grass so far being too short for feed, we bought hay from the farmers as we needed it. We had brought corn enough to last a few days. After a day or so of tolerable going the rain began again. Our teams were still raw and one yoke was newly broken, so that we were kept busy urging them through the mud.

At Chatfield, then a thriving inland village, we

bought corn enough to do us until feed should get better. Here we crossed Root river and entered a thick growth of oak timber. We traveled until night overtook us and made camp under the trees.

Early the next morning we were on our way, eager to reach the open again. Throughout the last mile of this woodland, which bordered upon Grand meadow, were the rookeries of countless numbers of passenger pigeons. Their myriad voices reached us in a low murmur, broken by the flapping of wings and the snapping of twigs long before we came in sight of them. When we drew near the air was fairly alive with the busy creatures, just now intent upon their nest building. Every tree, it seemed to me, held from three or four up to twenty-five or thirty nests in various stages of completion. These nests were shallow affairs, woven of sticks and lined. They would hold two or three eggs.

The passenger pigeon somewhat resembles its kinsman, the turtle-dove, in size and shape, with the exception that the tail of the passenger-pigeon is long and forked. The color is dull blue above, verging to a slightly reddish tinge below, with bright neck markings in the male. These colors and markings are less pronounced in the female. I have seen the air literally darkened for hours during their migrations. But the snare, the fowling-piece, and the squab hunter have done their work, and it is doubtful if any are left. The last one known of these interesting birds is said to have died in captivity at Cincinnati some years ago.

Our road now led gradually over low bluffs which marked the west boundary of Root river valley. Here the ten- or twelve-mile stretch of timber ended abruptly and we found ourselves upon the wide expanse of upland known as Grand meadow. With easier going we made the twelve-mile drive across in good season in spite of a recurrence of showers early in the day. At night we camped at the west edge of Grand meadow, not far from the Brownsdale settlement.

From here on to Albert Lea, nearly a three days' lap, we encountered scattered settlements along the streams and numerous lakes abounding in this region. Minnesota is unrivaled in the number and beauty of her lakes. They are said to be of glacial origin, and in their setting of boulders and virgin timber, they seemed themselves bits of the cloud-decked sky which they so clearly mirrored.

Just north of Albert Lea we camped on a small stream connecting two lakes. Here we saw a man taking fish out of a wooden trap placed at the head of a mill-race. Having filled a couple of buckets he told us to help ourselves, adding that he fed most of them to his hogs. There were suckers, buffalo-fish, and carp. We took some of the buffalo and carp to cook for supper. That evening Lon and I caught a good string of bullheads out of the upper lake. These bite well at night and are good eating.

At Albert Lea we laid in a supply of eggs at five cents a dozen. These we packed in oats and they lasted us several weeks.

Our two-day progress to Blue Earth City was without incident. We found plenty of wood, water, and grass and fair roads. We passed bubbling springs near the water-courses, many of which, when piped, rise to a height of several feet, forming the flowing wells so common here. There was a riot of wild flowers along the way, sweet peas, spring beauties, and shy wood violets, and in the low places purple flag and wild phlox. Curlews circled above us, uttering their plaintive call. Every once in a while one of them, resentful of our intrusion, would swoop down almost upon us, then dart away again to repeat the assault until we were clear of its premises. About the lakes were water-fowl in incredible numbers and variety, "so wild that they were tame." All day and far into the night the air was filled with their discordant cries. There seemed to be every variety of duck, most numerous of which were the mallard, the glossy green of their wings flashing in the sunlight. Besides these were the dusky river duck, teal, canvasback, and a little white fellow which I have often seen in the bayous of the lower Mississippi. Then there were the magnificient wood-duck, now so rare, with their tufted crests and brilliant markings.

Snow-white gulls with black feet and occasional black head-markings left their well-concealed nests in their quest for insects, worms, and other small game.

Impudent little helldivers would paddle around close by. I have often tried to hit them with pebbles, and never succeeded.

In going past a muskrat house or a pile of driftwood I was frequently startled by a mud-hen taking to the water with a squawk and a splash. After flopping noisily along the surface several rods, she would suddenly dive from sight or rise in swift flight.

There were squadrons of brant and wild geese. One of the geese, a large buff and light-gray bird, sent forth a sweet tremolo call greatly resembling the distant notes of a steamboat whistle.

Of that noblest of all water-fowl, the swan, there were two kinds, the "mute" swan and, more rarely, the trumpeter or "bugler," so called from its musical song while in flight. A good old lady of our neighborhood once hurried over to our house just at dusk, saying that she had seen a band of white-robed angels overhead, the leader of whom was blowing a trumpet. We were never able to convince her that what she had seen was only a flock of swan on one of their migrations, headed by their musical leader.

Along the lake shores we frequently saw pelicans stalking clumsily about, with their pouches so full of fish that they could hardly rise in the air. Skimming over the water or wading along the reedy margins were noisy killdeer, snipe, and sand-hill cranes. Blue herons flapped lazily overhead. Swallows and blackbirds were everywhere. Occasionally a fish-hawk, circling above the water, would dart with lightning rapidity upon some luckless fish that had come too near the surface and bear the struggling victim away in its claws.

I have often wondered how so many forms of bird life could exist peaceably in these aviaries provided by nature. If not on intimate terms of friendship, they at least preserved an armed neutrality until their young were reared and the time came to seek other haunts.

We had now reached the series of lakes known as the Chain lakes. We crossed the three chains, East, Center and West chain and soon found ourselves at the Iowa line. Transportation facilities only were needed to change this sparsely settled region of rich alluvial soil and favorable climate into a prosperous farming section. The day before we reached Estherville it began to rain again. We had not been on the road over an hour when we saw a heavily-loaded wagon without a cover, drawn by a gaunt team of horses. Two or three persons were walking beside the wagon. Before we caught up they had stopped, apparently mired down. When we drew near one of the horses was down and a boy about my own age was unhitching the other. The mother and smaller children were doing what they could to help. Leaving our teams, we all went over to give them a lift. Dad Ridgley unfastened the neckyoke of the fallen horse, Lon unhooked the tugs, and the deacon caught hold of a strap to lift by. The horse, evidently discouraged, seemed in no hurry to rise, in spite of all our tugging, pulling, and coaxing.

"Hit him, boy," shouted Deacon Smith. The boy obeyed with alacrity. But the deacon's hand lay in the general direction of the lash when it fell with a stinging blow. It was then that the good man used language. Before we all – the deacon included – had recovered from our amazement, the horse was up. We next put the forward ox-team to the wagon and drew it out of the mud-hole. Then we lightened the load by taking the mother and smaller children in our wagons; and as soon as the horses were in their traces again, we all proceeded together.

From Estherville we traveled westward through a thinly settled country, reaching East Okaboja lake two days later. Here midway of the east shore of the lake we came upon the home of our new acquaintances. Their house was substantially built of hewn logs, and together with a log barn and other buildings, stood in an enclosure of rails. They would not allow us to go on without visiting them there. So we decided to lay over the remainder of that day and the next. We learned in the course of our stay with this family, whose name was Francis, that the father had enlisted in a volunteer company of cavalry in the late summer of 1862, at the commencement of the indian uprising known as the

Minnesota massacre. He had sent his family to relatives near Madison, Wisconsin, where they remained through this trying period until now. His
term of enlistment instead of ending with the ces-
sation of indian hostilities as they had supposed,
would continue throughout the regular three-year
period. Believing the danger past, the family had
decided to come back to put in the crop and try to
make a go of things until the father's return. They
were gratified to find that nothing had been mo-
lested during their absence.

The day following our arrival, while the women
folk washed clothes and "cooked up," Dad Ridgley
and the deacon looked over the wagons and equipment, making repairs where needed. Some of the
oxen had rubbed sore spots on their necks. These
were treated with salve and the yokes scraped
smooth where they touched the shoulders.

After we had helped the women folk about the
house the oldest boy, Tom, and I went down to the
lake to fish and have a boat ride. On the way we
found his fish pole where he had cached it nearly
two years before. Then we brought the boat out
of its cache and had a good ride on the lake.

We all enjoyed eating at a table and living "like
white folks" once more. Yet it was characteristic
of Mrs. Ridgley and Mrs. Francis that, beyond de-
ploring the fact that they were as brown as gypsies
and that their hair would never come unsnarled,
they minimized the real discomforts of their jour-

ney. They were too busy making the best of things to repine.

The next morning we parted from the Francis family and started on our way. All of us, including the animals, were greatly refreshed after our layover.

We crossed a branch of the Little Sioux sometime during the day and the main stream the following day near where Peterson now stands. We found Cherokee to be a hamlet of two or three buildings and a gristmill. Here, after crossing the Little Sioux for the last time, we left the timbered region and struck into the military road leading westward across an unbroken prairie to the Floyd river, forty-five miles distant. The government wagons were all wide-tread, and as we traveled along, one side of our wagons would be in the rut and the other side on the center ridge, the oxen weaving from side to side in their effort to find better footing. It was a time to try the souls of men and oxen too. It wasn't long till I had yelled myself hoarse.

From the stunted appearance of the willows and other growth along the ravines we judged that prairie fires had been frequent.

About half way across, a band of elk, the first I had ever seen, bore down upon us from the north. They crossed the road at a shambling trot only a few rods ahead of us and disappeared over a knoll. Their leader was a magnificient bull, with velvet

stubs where his antlers had been a few weeks earlier. They were a pretty sight out there in the open.

Three days brought us across the prairie to the
Floyd, fifteen miles north of Sioux City. Here we
camped for the night. Next morning we crossed
the river and followed its course to the vicinity of
Sioux City, where we camped about a mile southeast of the town. Across the river about a mile
southeast of us we could see the white tents of General Sully's camp among the trees. We had reached our first objective.

Chapter III
Loading Up

Loading Up

It was now the thirtieth of May and we had made approximately three hundred miles. We had reached the highway of westward migration. Our next move was to seek admission to some emigrant party then forming. If successful we would finish our loading and be in readiness to go on. As before stated we were traveling light, having put in only such supplies as we might not get at any of the outfitting points on the Missouri. Besides dried fruits, cereals, beans, a few root vegetables, etc., Mrs. Ridgley had included a generous amount of home-canned products, mostly fruits. The greater part of this she had packed in a barrel, putting flour around each can to lessen the jar and keep them at a uniform temperature. There were also the bedding, tools, seeds and cuttings, a few indispensable pieces of furniture, some dishes, two window sash, a cook stove, the family Bible, and the clock; besides our personal effects, most of which we carried in seamless sacks with our initials on them.

We had been told that General Sully was organizing an expedition with the intention of laying out a new route up the north side of the Missouri as far as the present site of Bismarck, then across the river and westward through the Little Missouri

and Yellowstone regions, and on to the mines. At
his camp were two regiments of "Galvanized Yankees" to be used as escort. In the hope that we
might join this party, Dad Ridgley and Deacon
Smith visited Sully at his headquarters in Sioux
City. They found the General very difficult to approach just then, and were unable to make arrangements to go with him. Could we have foreseen
what lay in store for this expedition after it got
under way, we would have counted ourselves lucky
that we were not along. As it was Mr. Ridgley and
the deacon left the general's headquarters consid-
erably nettled and began making other plans.

In the meantime I was strolling along the main
street of the town when presently I heard a commo-
tion in front of a store. A little knot of spectators
had gathered about two men who were evidently
engaged in heated discussion. One was a tall, mus-
cular man of middle age, the other was a young
army officer of slighter build. As I drew near, a
big burly German private stepped between the
two and demanded of the civilian:

"Vot iss dot you say, Sir?"

"I say, Sir," replied the other, emphasizing his
words with a forefinger, "that the North will never
whip the South under the present administration,
Sir!"

At that the soldier struck him a blow right over
the left eye, peeling the skin back to the scalp and
knocking him cold.

Just then the storekeeper came out to see what

the row was about. Taking in the situation at a glance he went inside and returned with a basin of cold water which he dashed over the prostrate man. At the signs of returning consciousness they picked him up and carried him inside, the storekeeper remarking dryly:

"Maybe the damned old fool will know enough to keep his mouth shut after this."

The excitement being over I went back to camp.

When the men returned we talked over the matter of going on from here. The river route was considered out of the question on account of the excessively high rates and the difficulty of securing passage so far above Saint Louis, the usual loading point. Our best plan seemed to be to go on down to Council Bluffs, cross over to Omaha, and take the Platte route used by the Mormons in 1847-1848.

Of our six days' journey to Council Bluffs there is little to record. We passed Floyd's Bluff just above the present site of Sergeant Bluff, now a suburb of Sioux City. Floyd's Bluff, as well as the river and village, were named for Sergeant Charles Floyd, of the Lewis and Clark expedition, who died and was buried here in 1804. The bluffs at this point rise abruptly from the river. Formerly, and within the memory of men then living, quite a strip of level wooded plain intervened between the river and the bluffs.

The Missouri is at all times a turbulent stream, continually changing her channel. At this time of year, especially, her swollen and accelerated cur-

rent beats resistlessly against her yielding banks,
furnishing a striking example of the work of ero-
sion constantly going on.

Along the river bottoms and up the side streams
were scattering farms, many of them owned by
French-canadians who had trapped furs and traf-
ficked with the indians in earlier times, but were
now settled with their indian wives in the quieter
pursuits of farming.

During the forenoon of June 5, we reached Crescent City, about six miles northwest of Council
Bluffs. Here were a grist-mill and a good general
store, where prices were more reasonable than at
the larger outfitting points. Knowing also that it
would be easier to finish loading where there was
less confusion, we stopped and changed things
around in the wagons so as to put the stuff in. We
laid in flour enough to last us eighteen months, or
until the next year's crop should be harvested, and
a year's supply of bacon and lard, besides corn
meal, coffee, sugar, salt, and other articles. We
thought we could get potatoes out beyond Omaha
and thus save the extra hauling.

Our load completed, we crossed a low ridge and
drove down a small stream called Lousy creek.
Several converging roads had formed quite a
thoroughfare along this valley. It was said that
Lousy creek got its name from the fact that many
emigrants were accustomed to halt on its banks to
do their washing. We camped for the night out on
the bottom between Council Bluffs and the river.

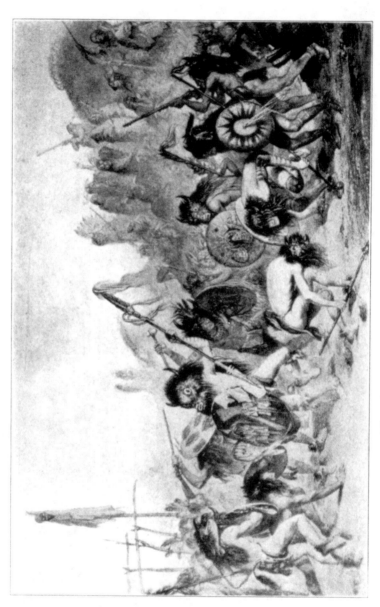

THE BUFFALO DANCE OF THE MANDANS
From an original drawing by Charles Bodmer about 1837

Council Bluffs had been the site of the Potawatomi indian agency until the late forties. The Mormons next came and tarried five years before going on to Utah, naming the place Kanesville. Later its present name was chosen to commemorate an important council which the Lewis and Clark party held with the indians in 1804. When we first saw Council Bluffs it was somewhat larger than either Sioux City or Omaha, and still enjoyed much of the overland trade begun during the California gold rush.

Chapter IV
Passing the Border

Passing the Border

On the following morning, June 6, we drove upon the ferry and were carried across to Omaha. At the wharf a boat load of goods from Saint Louis was being unloaded. Bales of dry-goods, hundred-pound sacks of sugar and "State" flour, bags of cured meats, coffee and dried fruits, cases of lard and molasses, casks of butter and salt-fish and various other staples were dumped unceremoniously upon the landing and promptly hauled away.

We picked our way along the deeply rutted main street through a tangle of traffic, reaching the business section more by the grace of God than by our skill in driving. Here were stores and warehouses combined, where goods were brought up from the wharves and reloaded into great freight wagons to supply the posts and other isolated points out on the trails or sold across the counter to a shifting crowd of emigrants, indians, and local residents.

Sounds of hilarity issued from the numerous saloons and dance halls, where strapping bullwhackers and muleskinners, during a carefree hour, were being adroitly relieved of their surplus cash through the agency of velvet-handed card experts or the age-old trinity, wine, women, and song.

Variously-clad papooses pressed grimy faces a-
gainst tempting show-windows, scurrying to cover
whenever some lusty reveler came striding uncer-
tainly along the sidewalk. Here and there a soldier
mingled with the crowd. Horses, mules, cattle,
dogs, the rumbling of wagons, the shouting of
drivers – all contributed to the general confusion.
It was altogether a situation that would have made
a traffic cop earn his money, had there been one.

Once clear of the jam we pulled out to where
the City hall now stands, followed the military
road northwest about five miles, and camped for
the night on the Papillion. Our camp was perhaps
a couple of miles southwest of the village of
Florence, where the Mormons made their winter
quarters in 1846.

Mr. Ridgley had bought a guide-book for thirty-
five cents at La Crosse before we started. Beginning at Omaha it indicated our route to the minut-
est detail, including not only the accurate location
of all landmarks, river crossings, posts, etc., but
directions about feed, water, and desirable camping places as well. The farther out we got, the
more we found it to our advantage to follow its
directions quite literally.

We were now on the northern branch of the
Overland trail, commonly called in these parts the
Mormon trail. Doctor Hebard in *The Bozeman
Trail* speaks of, "The indian road that was to be-
come the trail to the west for the white man, and
to be known as the Oregon trail, which the indians

in time called 'the Great Medicine Road of the Whites.' This trail was also known by the name of the Overland trail, the Mormon road, the Emigrant road, the Salt Lake route and the California trail." Thus you see it variously designated. Here the Mormons passed in 1848 to found an empire on the shores of Great Salt Lake; here also, the home-seeker, bound for Oregon and the forty-niner, caught by the lure of California gold.

The thirty-five mile trip from Omaha to Fremont consumed nearly three days. We crossed the Missouri river brakes and passed over rolling prairies, reaching the broad, level valley of the Elkhorn about ten miles east of Fremont. We found this stream easy to ford, and the road on to the Platte perfectly level. At Fremont, on the Platte, we camped on June 9. The town consisted of three stores and two or three other business places, besides about a dozen dwellings. The buildings were almost all of cottonwood logs. We were told that the store with the dirt roof and floor did the most business, and here we made our purchases.

Near Fremont a family by the name of Bouton, of Sioux City, added their two wagons to our little train. This family continued with us the greater part of the way across.

Our road now lay along the Platte. We were to follow this historic river for a distance of approximately seven hundred miles without leaving its banks for long. This stream throughout the

greater part of the year flows in small channels between numberless sandbars. The normal width in
its lower course often exceeds a mile. During the
spring freshets, however. it usually runs bank full.
For the greater part of its length it follows a fairly
straight course through a broad level flood plain,
furnishing probably the best natural route ever
used for overland travel.

We were four or five days on the road from Fremont to Columbus, then a town of about three hundred inhabitants. Here we expected to replenish
our supply of potatoes; but the demand had been
greater than the supply, and we could not get any
for love or money.

At Columbus we overtook three young men from
Iowa, who were on their way to Denver. Their
names were Joe Donovan, Tim Ware, and Billy
Moore. They had brought a hand shingle-mill
along, expecting to start up in business. This consisted of a frame fitted with a heavy blade, in
which a pine or cedar block, previously "slabbed
off" with a "frow" was set and riven into shingles
of the desired thickness. I struck up quite an inti-
macy with Joe Donovan, who was the youngest of
the three. Our train was now increased to six
wagons.

Just beyond Columbus we were taken part way
across the Loup river on a rope ferry and landed
on a sand bar from which we forded the rest of the
way across. The Loup, though much smaller than
the Platte, is a more sluggish stream and can rarely

The Sacred Buffalo Skull

be safely forded. A rope ferry, as we knew it, was a flatboat atttached by a short rope at either end to a pulley running on a cable stretched across the stream. To go forward the nearer pulley-rope was let out until the force of the current, striking the boat slantwise, would carry it along unaided. To return, the process was reversed.

Along the river were the cabins of a Pawnee indian village. These indians were friendly to the whites and were often employed as scouts and guides for the government. They had erected arbors in front of the cabins, covered with green branches, in whose shade they spent much of their time when at home. Although the indians themselves were rather sketchy as to personal appearance, their premises were quite tidy. It was amusing to watch the papooses paddling around in the water. They could swim like ducks. We heard their merry laughter as they splashed water on each other. The joy of childhood knows no race nor color.

About midway between Columbus and Grand Island we camped for the night on a small stream called the Rawhide. The story was then current that during the California gold rush, an emigrant party once camped here. Among them was a young fellow, thirsting for glory, who had vowed that he was going to shoot the first indian he saw. Against the protests of the others he got his indian – a defenseless squaw. When her people heard of the deed they surrounded the camp in great numbers

and demanded the guilty one, threatening to anni-
hilate the whole party unless he was produced. He
was promptly delivered into their hands. Then,
before the eyes of the horror-stricken white men,
the indians skinned their victim alive. This stream
has been known ever since as Rawhide creek.

Another day brought us to the head of Grand
Island. We had been traveling along this island at
least three days. The timber was heavy here; but
our guide book stated that we would encounter no
more trees for two hundred miles and that a sufficient quantity of wood should be laid in to last us
through this treeless region. We thereupon chop-
ped down a good-sized tree, which we sawed into
stove-lengths and split, putting as much as we
could get into the front end of each wagon. (We
used a small sheet-iron camp stove when it rained
or for baking; the rest of the time we cooked over
an open fire.) We then fastened a piece of timber
to the reach of my wagon.

Just across the river on the branch of the Overland trail which followed the south bank of the
Platte was Fort Kearney. We could not see it for
the timber. Fort Kearney, established in 1847, was
the first of a series of three forts – Kearney, Laramie, and Hall – established on the Overland trail
to protect emigration. These forts served as bases
for supplies and ammunition and headquarters for
the distribution of soldiers wherever needed. Telegraphic communication was maintained between
these forts and the intervening posts or stations, and

with Omaha and Fort Leavenworth through branch lines from Fort Kearney.

Here opposite the historic old fort we camped for the night. We were now fairly out upon the Great Plains.

Chapter V

From Fort Kearney to Fort Laramie

From Fort Kearney to Fort Laramie

Thus far I have sketched our trip in a somewhat cursory manner, taking very little account of the personal equation. This is partly owing to the fact that we had been passing through scenes which though trivial in themselves were ever new and changing. Now it was different. There were long days of dust, of increasing heat, of endless prairie. Deadly monotony that turned one's mind inward. Oxen are good, faithful creatures, but they *are* slow. Mrs. Ridgley said that her back ached riding all day in a wagon that jolted you to pieces every time you hit a stone. She didn't see how that poor woman in the wagon back of the deacon's could get along with a cross baby. And if one was a man one wouldn't have to sit cramped up all day and every day.

In mild defense of his sex Mr. Ridgley would reply that it wasn't exactly easy to walk halfway across the continent alongside of a team of oxen with a yoke of steers in the center that you had to keep watching continually. At which his good wife would smile a little wearily. *She* knew who had the hardest part of the bargain, etc.

But when camp was made and the grub-box and cooking things were set out, Mrs. Ridgley would cook such good things to eat that we would all straightway forget the discomfort of the day's travel.

We were now adding to our train. During the week following our camp opposite Fort Kearney we numbered a dozen wagons in all. Human nature was the same then that it is now. People *would* disagree. Wagons from other parties fell in with us, perhaps because of uncongenial associates, perhaps because of a difference in the rate of speed in traveling.

It was along here that we began to put out night guards. Roving bands of indians were becoming frequent. They were ostensibly hunting, but we suspected that they would not be above helping themselves to some "slow elk." I took my turn with the rest on the day and night shifts. Day shift was from the time we turned out till nine o'clock in the evening; night shift from nine till four next morning. Later we put on two night shifts, one from nine till twelve, the other from twelve till four. When not standing night guard I was called at four in the morning to run in the cattle. In a fit of self pity I considered myself the small boy that was given the dull hoe and told to keep up.

However, an incident occurred which was to change things somewhat. We had camped one night about half way between Grand island and the junction of the North and South Platte rivers. It was a very sultry evening and the mosquitoes were out in full force. Joe Donovan and I were detailed to hold guard that night. We had to take the cattle away from the bottom into the low range of hills bordering the valley about two miles north of camp. The understanding was that if anything happened and we needed help we were to fire a shot and they would all come to our aid. After the cattle had lain down for the night we went in among them and sat down to while away the hours with yarns. Under the influence of the moonlight and the drowsy stillness we gave free rein to our fancy. It was my turn, and I related the following story which Dad Ridgley had told around the campfire at home:

"Back at Fort Bedford, Pennsylvania, in early day, the supply of meat was running low. Settlers who had sought protection at the fort reported that they could hear a wild turkey gobble out in the timber. Wild turkeys were plentiful in those days, and a fellow volunteered to go out and get this one. He didn't come back. Another fellow went out, and he didn't come back. The third day an old indian fighter happened at the fort. When he heard the turkey gobble again he said,

" 'I'll go and get that turkey.'

"He went out with his gun and soon came back with his game – a buck indian. That stopped the gobbling."

Just then a coyote set up a howl a little way off. We had never heard a coyote and it startled us. Joe said,

"Do you suppose that's indians hollering to get us out where they can shoot us?"

"I don't know," I answered.

Joe had a double-barreled shot-gun and I had a big six-shooter.

"Can you work it?" asked Joe.

"Oh, yes," I answered; "it works just this way." With that I pulled up one trigger and must have accidentally touched the other, for at that instant the gun went off with a tremendous roar right in among the cattle. They didn't even get up to see what had happened. But the coyote stopped howling. We were now afraid that everybody would be up from camp. A half hour passed; an hour. No one showed up. Next morning, as we were driving the cattle back to camp, we scared up a coyote.

"I'll bet that's the one that howled last night," Joe exclaimed.

When they heard about our experience at camp Dad Ridgley let me off from night duty, saying that I was too young to be out all night that way, anyhow.

In another day or so a wagon drawn by two yoke of steers and a yoke of heifers pulled in with us. There were four men in the outfit from Raleigh, Missouri. One of their number, George Colburn, had been out on the plains seven years.

Our supply of wood was now getting pretty low. To make it last till we should reach timber again we took sacks and skirmished around for buffalo chips. We would have to begin early as they were scarce around the camp grounds. I got a little driftwood off from tow-heads in the river; but the current was usually so swift along here that it was hardly worth while trying to drag it ashore. I had swum the cattle over to a small island where feed was good one evening and was trying to salvage a few pieces of driftwood, when a small flatboat came floating by. I jumped in after it and managed to steer it ashore. As I neared the river bank two of the fellows from camp stood with their guns pointed in my direction. They explained that an indian might have been hidden in the boat ready to scalp me, and they weren't going to take any chances. We couldn't use the boat, so I tied it up there, thinking that somebody might need it.

We were meeting people every day. Some of them brought reports of trouble with the indians. There were persistent rumors of stage-coaches and trains being raided, of horses stolen, of telegraph wires cut and matters of a more serious nature. It seemed that the indians wanted horses more than anything else – horses, guns, and ammunition. We had no horses. There was no cause to worry on that account. Nevertheless, though no one would have admitted it, we all began to feel "keyed up."

By the time we reached the junction of the Platte, Mrs. Ridgley announced that we had used the last of the potatoes. Except for a few onions, we were without fresh vegetables of any kind, and no prospects of getting any along the road. Cases of scurvy due to the lack of fresh vegetables were

common. Among our supplies were dried pumpkin, sweet-corn, apples, and peaches. There were
also home-canned tomatoes, preserves, and jam
sealed in tin. With a constant supply of fresh milk
and occasional messes of wild greens and small
fruit – when we were lucky enough to find any
that had been missed – we kept our rations fairly
well balanced and were never troubled with scurvy.
Alonzo, the hunter, kept us supplied with game.

Of every party we met we inquired for news of
the Philipps boys. Apparently no one had seen
them. Finally one day we spied a cleft stick driven
into the ground by the side of the road, bearing a
folded bit of paper. No one ever looked for the
letter carrier more eagerly than emigrants did for
these wayside message-bearers. And how carefully the notes were replaced if they chanced to be for
somebody else! Out where there was no law, this
was the unfailing custom.

Mr. Ridgley was the first one to the note. He
could not read, but his wife could. It was addressed to us and was from the Philipps brothers. It
stated that they had passed here a week earlier and
urged us to catch up with them if possible, ending
with, "Both well – Philipps Boys." This was a
cheerful diversion.

We passed the forks of the river and would now
follow the North Platte. The Overland road on
the south side of the river divided at this point.
One branch crossed the South Platte and paralleled the North Platte opposite us, merging with our

The Willow Dance of the Cheyennes

road at Platte Bridge, above Fort Laramie; the other followed the upward course of the South Platte, past the present site of Fort Collins, Colorado, and swinging north-westward, joined the northern branch of the road a little way east of Fort Bridger. This was known as the Overland Stage route.

One evening as I was holding the herd over next the bluffs out of sight of camp, two mounted indians came tearing down the slope in my direction, laying the quirt on their ponies and ki-yi-yipping like sixteen to the dozen. Almost upon me, they drew their mounts to their haunches, demanding gruffly,

"Where your tepee?"

"Yonder," I answered in as big a voice as I could command; "Where's your tepee?"

They pointed across the river, looked at each other a minute and grinned; then putting quirt to their ponies again, they wheeled and rode off, yelling as before. I wondered to myself if they saw how my knees were trembling. Perhaps they thought I was too small game.

More heat, clouds of acrid dust, mosquitoes, cactus, prairie-dogs, horned-toads, rattlesnakes – and the endless plain. How the wheels of some old linch-pin wagon would "holler" for tar from the bucket hanging in the rear. The oxen were suffering from the heat, and we began giving them longer noons and traveling earlier and later. We also corraled when we camped.

One day ahead of us, apparently right in the road, a slender spire made its appearance. It grew daily larger, until now at our left it stood out upon the bluff across the river, a solitary shaft of sand rock towering two-hundred feet or more above its conical base. Chimney Rock our guide book called it. We were told that some years earlier a company of soldiers out on target practice had turned a small cannon upon it, breaking off about thirty feet of its top.

Mirages became frequent. To one not accustomed to these phenomena, the sudden appearance against the horizon of trees, antelope, and other objects, weirdly distorted and in grotesque attitudes, was invariably a scource of wonder. The initiated were always ready to be amused at the novice's expense.

The next important landmark was Scott's Bluff, on the same side of the river, a good day's journey from Chimney Rock. It is also of sand rock and towers above its fellows like a ruined castle. A scattering growth of cedar softens its rugged outlines.

Along here about camping time we met a party of three wagons, who stopped and asked if they might camp with us. We were always glad to meet people from out west; it was about our only way of finding out what was going on ahead of us. So we all camped together. In the course of the evening they told us that they were Mormon converts who had eluded the "Avenging Angels" and at great peril to themselves had escaped from Salt Lake City, after living under conditions that had grown intolerable to them there. They looked to us as though they had suffered untold hardships.

Two days' drive east of Fort Laramie, about nine o'clock in the morning as we were just starting, a company of soldiers forded the river from the south and rode over toward us. They greeted us cordially and soon were scattered along the line in lively conversation with our people. The lieutenant told us that they were out on a scouting trip. He wanted to know if we would sell them some eatables – anything that would vary the monotony of their army rations of hardtack, bacon, beans, and coffee.

Mrs. Ridgley got out a can of her famous jelly. This, with articles gathered from the other wagons, they stored away in their saddle bags; and with a cheery "Good luck to you!" they cantered on northward toward the Niobrara river brakes. They were a gallant band on their prancing bays, the metal of their trappings flashing in the sunlight.

Next day on nearing Fort Laramie we got the story of what happened. A couple of hours after leaving us the lieutenant and two or three of his command were riding in advance up a narrow ravine when they ran into an ambush. Arrows came whizzing from both sides. The lieutenant fell from his horse, pierced through the neck. His comrades came on at top speed, routed the indians, and recovered their leader. They cut the arrow in

two and drew out the pieces. His last words were:
"The damned rascals have got my horse!"

For several days we had noted a tiny mound
of hazy blue like a distant haystack up the trail
ahead of us. We saw nothing in our guidebook to
enlighten us. Gradually it grew larger until finally we could distinguish the outlines of a snow-
clad mountain crest. It was Laramie peak.

Our train by this time numbered about twenty-
seven wagons. Within half a day's drive from Fort
Laramie we came upon a large indian village.
They were mostly Sioux, with a sprinkling of
Cheyennes and Arapahoes. We were told that
there were at least two thousand indians encamped
in the vicinity of Fort Laramie that year. This
was probably their largest village. The whole flat
for nearly a mile between us and the river was covered with their lodges, set regularly in rows facing
upon the several streets. The lodges were of sum-
mer-killed elk or buffalo hides and would hold
fifteen or twenty persons ordinarily. They were
fancifully decorated with paintings in vivid
colors, representing scenes of prowess, in which
mounted Sioux were killing incredible numbers
of Crows or bagging quantities of big game, which
never for long eluded their skill. Smoke curled
lazily from a few scattering camp fires in front of
the lodges.

Indians of all degrees, ages, and sexes left their
occupation and hurried out to the road to have a

INTERIOR OF THE WILLOW DANCE TEPEE

look at us, as we stopped for a few moments. Here were the pride and flower of the plains, indians in all their glory. Some were *en déshabillé*; others were the pride and flower of the plains indians in varying notions of comfort; while still others, having apparently exhausted the resources of their own wardrobes, had borrowed extensively from various sources. There was much individual choice in the matter of head covering. The women, when they wore anything on their heads at all, seemed to prefer gaudily colored silk handkerchiefs as best suited to set off their charms. Some of the men sported hats of various styles. Blankets and shawls were of every variety of color and material. Some were of light canvas, others of thick wool. One old squaw was proudly draped in the folds of a red checked tablecloth. The faces and hair partings of some of the women were touched up with vermillion and yellow ocher. The hair of both men and women was done in two braids, almost invariably ornamented with small white shells or beads. Their ears were pierced – in many cases slit – and hung with silver and brass earrings and pendants. There was great display of finger rings and bracelets.

A tall, stately indian now came clanking up in an officer's cast-off uniform, with a sword at his side. A young fellow of our party stepped forward and asked to see the sword. The indian, with great ostentation, drew it from its scabbard and handed it to him. The sword was duly examined, admired, and returned to its owner, who, sliding it back into the scabbard, demanded,

"Hap a dollah."

The young fellow, perhaps not taking him seriously, replied,

"No see um half a dollar."

The indian uttered a derisive "Yee! Yee!" and strode off in high dudgeon, his pig tails bobbing beneath his enormously high-crowned hat.

After we had pulled on a mile or so a string of packers told us that about a hundred miles back indians had killed an emigrant and driven off his horses. Further questioning brought out the fact that the man's name was Farnham, of La Crosse, and that he was bound for the goldfields with a couple of wagon loads of merchandise. It was our Farnham, without doubt, the same who was to have gone with us but for delays in getting his loads ready. It seemed that he had gone down to the river a couple of hundred yards below camp to water his teams, when an indian sprang from cover and grabbed the halter ropes. Farnham grappled with him, but the indian was too nimble. Whipping out a revolver, he blew Farnham's head off and escaped with the horses before any one from camp could intervene.

That evening we camped about three miles below Fort Laramie. Double guards with extra guns and ammunition watched that night.

Chapter VI

The Alder Clump Springs Detour

The Alder Clump Springs Detour

Early in the forenoon of July 3, we were opposite Fort Laramie. Here were more indians with their customary display of borrowed (or stolen) finery and native curiosity. They made great show of friendship; yet we could not help noting the almost total absence of warriors among them. There seemed to be only the older men and the women and children around the camps. Unlike the eastern indians they did not offer to swap their wares. What attraction Fort Laramie had for them we could only conjecture. Perhaps it was the lure which a military post has always held for the roving classes. Perhaps they were maneuvering to get Uncle Sam to grant them annuities.

A mile further and we came to a temporary shelter of boards at the left of the road where an officer and his assistant were keeping a record of the traffic. They told us that, to date, upwards of six thousand wagons had passed westward over this road. A tally of the traffic was also kept on the south side of the river, which showed a total of over four thousand wagons so far. They judged that we were now midway of the emigration for that season.

We waited at the ford while some of the men,

including Dad Ridgley, waded across to visit the fort. The water was waist deep and rather swift, and each man cut a staff to support him in crossing. The road led them about a mile and a half down the opposite side to where the fort stood a short distance above the mouth of Laramie river, on the right bank. During their absence we amused ourselves by watching a small crowd of touseled indian boys in hickory shirts who were practicing with their bows and arrows on anything that would serve for targets. One of the soldiers set up a stick for a target, allowing each boy one hit out of every three shots to win a hardtack for his prize. Some of the fellows in our outfit dug into their boxes of hardtack to help the sport along.

The men returned from the fort, and we started on. While there, they made some purchases at the sutler's store kept by Seth Bullock. Many years later I came to know Mr. Bullock in the Black Hills where he was engaged in the mercantile business in Deadwood and conducted a freighting enterprise in connection, between that point and Fort Pierre. From the comments of the men I gathered that Fort Laramie must have been a lively place, frequented by indians, emigrants and transients of all classes. The original fort, we were told, had been built just thirty years earlier by the Rocky Mountain Fur Company to control the fur-trade of the Arapahoes, Sioux, and Cheyennes. It was named for Jacques Laramie, a fur-trader. It was later taken over by the American Fur Company.

FORT LARAMIE, WYOMING
As it appeared in the sixties

In 1849 it was purchased by the government and removed to its present site. Eventually it grew into an eight-company post. In the days of the fur-traders it was a little adobe-walled fort with towers for defense at two opposite corners, separate enclosures for stock and the housing of people and goods, and a great entrance of heavy timbers, fitted with a small paneled opening. Here in the winter time were congregated Americans, Frenchmen, Spaniards, and Mexicans, with their indian wives and half-breed children. For the following account of old Fort Laramie I am indebted to Mr. John Hunton, of Torrington, Wyoming, who has been a resident of Fort Laramie and vicinity since the spring of 1867. Mr. Hunton's intimate knowledge of the development of the West and his willingness at all times to assist in securing data, have been of inestimable value to those who have attempted to preserve what is still available of pioneer material.

OLD FORT LARAMIE

"Tradition says Fort Laramie first became a rendezvous for white trappers sometime between 1815 and 1820, and that about that time Jules La Ramire was living and trapping in that section of country. Many things and places were given his name. It is supposed that he was killed by Arapahoe indians about 1820. He is now referred to as 'Jacques Laramie.' A few scattering trappers occupied the country for some years and early in the thirties a fur-trading post was established. In 1834 Sublett, Campbell and Bridger established a regular fur-trading post, the name of which was changed a number of times as different companies or individuals owned it. In June, 1849, the United States bought the buildings from the fur company, and on the twelfth of August, 1849, Company 'G,' 6th United States infantry, Captain William Kitcham, occupied it as a permanent garrison. It was occupied as a military post until April 20, 1890. During the Civil war the garrisons were mostly volunteer soldiers from different states, but from early in 1866 to abanonment there were none but regulars – cavalry or infantry. Some of the early buildings were constructed of adobe with dirt roof and the earth for floor. In course of time other and better buildings were constructed – large warehouses, shops, stables, bake house, and all necessary buildings for the use of the soldiers.

"For about thirty years after the post was first established all water used was hauled from the Laramie river in tank wagons and distributed to companies and to families by being taken from the tanks in buckets and emptied into barrels and such other containers as were used by the consumers. Along in the early eighties a good water system was constructed by which water was conducted to and through all buildings and to irrigate the parade ground. This water system was abolished when the fort was abandoned.

"Very many stirring scenes and incidents occur-

OLD FORT LARAMIE, WYOMING
As it appeared in the seventies

red at and near the fort during its existence, more particularly during the time that the indians were in the country. The indians never did attack the fort but for many years they kept it in a state of serious apprehension. From 1864 to 1877 it was quite unsafe to travel alone over any part of this country. There was generally kept at the fort during that period from 300 to 500 soldiers."

In the late afternoon we camped at a point where the road left the Platte for a time and skirted a range of hills cut by deep ravines. According to our guide book we would have a couple of days of exceedingly rough going and it would be well to look to our wagons and equipment before attempting it. We therefore decided to lay over the next day. It would be a pleasant place to spend the fourth.

Mr. Ridgley had always seen to it that the oxen received the best of care, and as a result they were in fine condition. Here we were halfway to our destination and not one of them had gone lame. Whenever any of them showed signs of becoming footsore we cut out pieces of sole-leather, one for each "toe," and fastened them on with oxshoe nails. We did not carry any iron shoes along, the leathers usually lasting as long as they were needed.

There was good feed here and we turned the cattle loose near camp, after which some of us went fishing and the rest busied themselves with the usual camp routine till supper-time. Soon George Colburn struck out in the direction of the old La

Bonte station up the river above Bridger's Ferry. When he didn't show up that evening we asked his companions where he had gone. They said they didn't know; and as they showed no concern about his absence, we let the matter drop for the time.

At sunset we heard the cannon booming at Fort Laramie.

The next morning at sunrise we were awakened by the same signal. The day passed quietly and pleasantly. We spent the forenoon greasing the wagons, tightening bolts, putting leathers at the ends of loose spokes next the fellies to tighten the wheels, and getting everything ready for a rough piece of road. Clothes were washed and hung on ropes stretched between the wagons or on convenient bushes. There were baking, churning, mending, and all the usual domestic activities of a large household. Everybody was talking at once. The children, rejoicing in their freedom, spent much of their time chasing indians on stick horses, followed by a pack of excited dogs. A returning fisherman brought in some pieces of rock which Dad Ridgley declared to be iron ore.

"Some day they'll be getting iron out of these hills," he said. "This rock looks just like what we had back there in Pennsylvany. The land in this country will never be good for nothing but grazing, though; it lays pretty enough, but it's too dry to farm."

As I was strolling along the road a little way north of camp I came upon another note from the

Philipps boys. It was dated a week earlier and stated a man named Bozeman was gathering up a train for the purpose of laying out a new road to Virginia City by way of the east side of the Big Horns, and that they were going to try to get in with them. The note was eagerly read at camp and the hope was expressed that we might be able to overtake the Bozeman party and thereby make a saving of nearly half of the distance to be traveled and at the same time avoid crossing the continental divide twice.

On the fifth we resumed the trail. George Colburn had not come back yet. As we neared the hill country we saw some heavy pieces of furniture cast out by the roadside. This was no new occurrence, however, as we had frequently seen chairs, bedsteads, or other articles along the way, warped by exposure to the elements. Mrs. Ridgley exclaimed over an escritoire of rare workmanship, and pitied the poor woman who had to part with it.

Before we reached Alder Clump springs, where we were to camp for the night, George Colburn rode up from the southwest on a United States mule with government saddle and bridle. He explained that he had bought the outfit. We knew the government wasn't selling mules or horses; they were needed too badly. And furthermore the brand on this one had not been "vented," so that it could not have been a legal transfer anyway. We were reminded of an incident that had occurred earlier, near the forks of the Platte. Colburn re-

turned one day from a similiar absence, riding a
saddle-horse which he claimed he had bought from
a fellow badly in need of money. He asked me con-
fidentially if I would be willing to swear to the
transaction if the occasion arose. To this I could
not think of agreeing. When later the owner rode
up and recognized the horse, assuming that it must
have been picked up as a stray, Colburn stoutly
protested that he had bought the animal from
another fellow. The quarrel which ensued had not
gone beyond the word stage when Mr. Ridgley,
sensing trouble, walked back and told Colburn
he'd better give up the horse. Seeing himself without support, Colburn did so with an ill grace, and
the owner, thankful to recover his property so easi-
ly, left without pushing the matter further. And
now that history seemed to be repeating itself, I
wondered what would be the outcome.

After a drive which taxed the endurance of the
oxen and ourselves as well we made camp at Alder
Clump springs, in an upland pass a little better
than midway of our detour from the river. The
springs bubbled up clear and cold from their sandy
depths and united to form a sparkling rivulet along
whose banks numerous thickets of alders con-
trasted the dark glossy green of their foliage with
the red-tinted crags and the purple sage.

I took the cattle down about a mile south of the
springs where the feed was good. George Colburn
joined me shortly. After a while we grew thirsty

JOHN SUBLETTE (left) TRAPPER, SCOUT, AND GUIDE

and I went up to camp for a canteen which I filled
at the springs and brought back to the herd with
me.

"Something queer happened while you was
gone," said George, after he had taken a drink
from the canteen.

"What was it?" I asked.

"W'y them damn fool Missourians that's camped down yender west of the road hev let ther hosses stampede. I counted twenty-one head an' a colt.
They'll claim that injuns hev run 'em off, an' they'll
be scairt to go after 'em. I'll go out in the mornin'
an' git some of them hosses 'fore night."

I could make out signs of confusion at the camp.
However, some distance beyond, a herd of mixed
stock seemed to be feeding quietly enough, and to
this I called his attention.

"It ain't them," he explained; "it was a bunch
of hosses over on this side along the ravine."

I had not noticed them myself. So they had
stampeded of their own accord, and it was to be
a case of "finders keepers" with Colburn. Different localities bred different morals, apparently.

Toward supper time, as we drove the stock up
nearer camp, I felt a growing curiosity to know
whether Colburn was telling the whole truth or
not. I would ask Lon and Joe what they thought
about it.

When we went in for supper we were told that
men from the other camp had just been there and

reported that indians had made a raid on their horses and driven off fourteen head. The horses were grazing just east of the wagons when a band of indians rode over a ridge and dashed between them and the camp. Beating upon dry hides, rattling small bells, and whooping and yelling, they stampeded the horses northwest toward the high hills. They kept at the rear, leaning over on one side of their horses so as to be invisible to the emigrants; and before the latter could reach their guns and bring them to bear, the redskins were well out of range of their old cap-and-ball rifles and were soon lost to sight among the brakes. An old man of the party had lost two teams and a saddle pony – all the stock he had. As there seemed to be no use trying to recover the stolen animals out in the rough country, handicapped as they were by a lack of saddle horses, they had decided to rearrange the loads, throw out what they couldn't carry, and divide up the stock so that all could go on.

That evening a meeting was held in our corral to which our friends from Raleigh, Missouri, were not invited. Colburn's story was compared with the emigrants' account. His former suspicious behavior and that of his companions was discussed; the mysterious absences; the horse deal; the army mule; and now – this. Clearly they were not to be trusted; and Colburn himself we now fully believed to be in league with the indians. There were many such renegade whites along the trails at that time who were perfectly at home among the indians and would steer "business" in their direction for a share in the gain. Their pay might be in money, furs, plunder, or a part of the stolen stock. Before the meeting broke up some one was instructed to inform these men of our unanimous decision that they must leave next day.

We kept the cattle near camp that night and put out double guards.

Early next morning Colburn saddled the mule, put a large pack behind the saddle, and rode off into the hills in the direction taken by the indians the afternoon before. A little later his companions drove on up the road. We never saw them again.

We took our own time about starting. When we passed the spot where the neighboring camp had been, there was nothing left but the ashes of extinguished camp fires and some household goods strewn about.

We made the eighteen-mile drive to the river before dark and camped a little way west of the present site of Orin junction, at a point near the intersection of our road and a branch of the Overland trail which crossed at Bridger's Ferry, a half day's drive down the river. We were all a little solemn that evening, for on the morrow Joe Donovan and his companions, who had won our friendship during the weeks of travel together, were leaving on the southward trail.

Our detour northward had given us a glimpse of the indians' favorite hunting grounds, roughly designated as the Powder river country; we were at the edge of "Indian Fairyland." Certainly an inhospitable region for emigrants.

Chapter VII
Where Trails Divide

Where Trails Divide

The next day, July 7, about the middle of the forenoon as we were passing over the ground where Douglas now stands, we noted the deep imprint of wagon wheels turning due north at right angles to our trail. Beside the road at our left was another note on a cleft stick from the Philipps brothers, stating that they were going with Bozeman by this new route that he was laying out to Virginia City and urging us to catch up with them if possible. The message bore the date of July 1. Here we halted until afternoon, turning the problem over in our minds, whether to follow Bozeman's party or stick to the old trail. There would be a great saving of time and ox-flesh by the new and shorter route east of the Big Horns. To avoid crossing and re-crossing the continental divide was itself a matter worth serious consideration, not to mention intervening stretches of desert waste to traverse. Yet it might have taken weeks to overtake the Bozeman train; and the growing hazard of traveling in small parties through the indian country alone outweighed all the advantages. We reached our decision and by one o'clock we had passed the Bozeman cut-off and were on our way up the Platte road.

After we had camped that evening a party with

horse teams travelling light informed us that on the preceding evening indians had raided another camp at Alder Clump springs, taking five mules and horses. Two men, it seems, had been holding a mixed herd about a quarter of a mile from their camp. They were leading the horses and mules back nearer camp when a lone indian walked up to them with a friendly greeting and shook hands with them. Then suddenly drawing his bow, he drove an arrow into the shoulder of one of the men, seized the halter-ropes as he fell, snatched the ropes from the other, who had but one arm and could not defend himself, mounted one of the animals and was beyond pursuit with his spoil in almost no time. This rough country seemed to be a favorite lurking place for indians. Reports of their depredations reached us daily, and we were never free from apprehension. We passed several newly-made graves.

Another day's travel brought us opposite Platte Bridge station. Our trail followed the bench to the north, and below us was the little stockaded post near the end of a long bridge of logs laid upon rock-filled log piers across the Platte. Here the telegraph line crossed and troops were stationed to help meet the growing need for protection against indian treachery. Mail, stage-coaches, freighters, and a stream of emigration passed here, and upon this point the indians were apparently directing their attention. Squads of soldiers were constantly patrolling the country or repairing telegraph wires mysteriously cut and were never far from the emigrant trains.

A report now reached us of a battle between the indians and a large emigrant party down on the Leavenworth trail. Of this incident Mrs. Anna Birlew, a neighbor, has the following to say:

"I remember as though it were yesterday the long ox-train as it passed through Geneva, Kansas, where we were then living. They had made up between Humboldt and Leroy. Mrs. Fannie Kelly and her husband and a little niece – I knew them well – joined them here. The day was so hot and sultry and as they crept along, the oxen lolling out their tongues, I had a presentiment that some danger lay in wait for them.

"Away out on the trail to the northwest somewhere it was that they had coraled for the night, when indians swooped down upon them with their blood-curdling warwhoops. Of the prisoners taken all got away, I believe, except Mrs. Kelly and her little niece – a sister's child left in her care – and another lady. As the indians marched along with their prisoners Mrs. Kelly contrived to leave the little girl beside the path, concealed among some tall grass and bushes, bidding her remain hidden until they were all out of hearing, then make her way back to the road where someone might see her and pick her up.

"The child left her hiding place and wandered on, at last reaching a knoll where she stood waving her hands and calling for help. Passing soldiers saw her from a distance, but fearing that she might be a decoy leading to an ambush, they waited some time before approaching. When they rode up to her, her lifeless body was pierced with arrows.

"Mrs. Kelly's companion made her escape a day or two later. Mrs. Kelly herself remained in captivity about two years. She was subsequently ransomed by the government. After her return to civilization she wrote a book in which she recounted her experiences while a captive."

When the report of this affair reached our home section in Wisconsin it had become distorted past recognition. Mrs. Ridgley was a prisoner among the savages; the rest of us had perished at their hands. It was six months before Mrs. Ridgley's daughter and my mother learned differently. Such was the prevalence of rumors in those days and the difficulty of correcting them.

Somewhere between Platte Bridge and the Sweetwater, we learned later, Jim Bridger, the famous scout and plainsman, had recently left our trail with an emigrant party bound for the mines by a route which he had selected northward through the Big Horn Basin and westward through Bozeman pass. It seemed that Bridger had chosen this route as being more practical and offering less danger from indian attack than that east of the Big Horns. We had heard a great deal of Bridger on our journey – of his ability as a scout and guide, his integrity and the esteem in which he was held

by the government and by private expeditions
which he had guided. His knowledge of the topog-
raphy of the country and his understanding of
indian methods of warfare were unequaled in any
other man, it was said.

We were now gradually reaching a higher level
and the oppressive heat of midsummer was consid-
erably modified by cool breezes from the snow-
clad mountains. In the late afternoon of July 12,
we came to Independence rock. It stands apart
from the nearby mountains – then known as the
Rattlesnake range – as though flung by a giant
hand out upon the plain. "The Great Register of
the Desert," Father De Smet called it. Our road
skirted the north side of the rock and some of us
got out to add our names to the many thousands
inscribed upon its western face. Here the rock
rises sheer to a considerable height, perhaps a hundred feet or more, receding inward toward the
base and effectually protecting the inscriptions
from the elements. Many of the names were car-
ved high above our heads. I still remember the
signatures of Kit Carson and generals Harney, Fremont, and Kearney.

We drove southward perhaps half a mile and
camped on a small stream. The little station which
we knew as Independence Rock post (Sweetwater
station) stood a short distance northeast of us. This
seemed to be a favorite camp ground. There were
several small outfits and a large camp within sight
of us.

I took the cattle out that evening and came back at dusk, having been relieved by Lon for the night shift. Somewhat later we were awakened from our slumber by approaching hoof beats and the clanking of a sabre. It proved to be an officer from the station who called out to us that he had just received a wire from Platte Bridge station ordering him to assemble all outlying trains at one point for defense. Mr. Ridgley replied that, dark as it was, it would be a difficult matter to fetch the cattle, which were out with the night herder.

"I'll go over to the large camp and see if I can get oxen there," returned the officer. And before he left he detailed briefly what had occurred. Over the wires had come the message that a battle had been fought with the indians that afternoon near Platte Bridge, fifty miles distant. The indians had been routed and were headed in this direction. Scattered trains, as before stated, were to be brought together and arrangements made for defense. Just as this message was being ticked off a young Arapahoe girl sought admission to the station and in broken English told the soldiers that the indians were preparing to attack the garrison and outlying trains at daybreak. Her mission of salvation accomplished, she slipped away in the darkness to her waiting horse as silently as she had come.

The young officer galloped down to the big train and soon men with oxen were on their way to pull us down there. Within an hour all the trains were merged in one immense corral, the wagons as they were driven into place being fastened together with four chains apiece. This done, a meeting was called and put in charge of a veteran army officer who chanced to be among the emigrants. Under his direction an estimate was made of the number of fighting men and the amount of guns and ammunition available. Soon upwards of two hundred resolute backwoodsmen stood armed and ready for orders. Next, portions of the loading within the wagons were shifted against the exposed sides as additional protection. Guards were then stationed at various points and all others sought the greater safety of their wagons, to be on the alert at a moment's notice. All of us, old and young, realized that a few short hours might bring death or worse, as in the case of other parties before us; yet I do not recall that there was a moment's panic that night.

While the sentinels watched, the hours slipped by, and morning was well along before I opened my sleep-clogged eyes and crawled out of my wagon. The others were up before me and breakfast was cooking. Lon had been relieved and was snoring in his wagon. I felt a little disappointed, after all our preparations, that no indians had showed up. I was certain that I could have done some execution with our old double-barreled shotgun.

We waited till ten o'clock, but there was no sign of indians. Had their spies noted our preparations in the night watches? Were the soldiers too hot on their trail? We never knew. Yet, had the "singing wires" snapped that night before the message came from Platte Bridge station, we might all have perished but for a little indian maid who risked her life to warn the pale-faces of their danger.

Everyone was now growing impatient of further delay, and it was decided to break corral. Slowly the great circle straightened out into a line which took half an hour to pass a given point. We were near the end and it seemed as though we would never get started. At last we were unwound like a gigantic game of crack-the-whip and began to move forward.

For an hour or so we traveled on a level; then we came to a steep hill. Here it was necessary to put on the rough locks, since emigrant wagons were seldom fitted with brakes. I shall never forget what a tedious experience this was. Every wagon had to wait until the one ahead was out of the way; otherwise, if a chain accidentally came loose, somebody was due for a big jolt.

Finally we got the wagons safely down and had lined them up on the flat below preparatory to unyoking for dinner, when some straggler cried out, "Indians!"

In less time than it takes to tell it, men and boys were assigned to hold the teams, one to every two or three wagons, while the others, guns in hands, were on their way to meet the enemy. Two spirited

Missouri girls, whose curiosity overcame their timidity, joined them. A couple of young fellows advised them to go back, urging that it was no safe place for women.

To which the girls replied, "When the rest retreat we will."

The young fellows grew emphatic. But what could you do?

The upshot of the matter was that when the defense party reached the brow of the hill, the girls were among the first.

Out upon the plain approaching riders were raising a cloud of dust. Back at the wagons those who had remained held fast to their courage and waited.

A few minutes, and what had been mistaken for indians proved to be a squad of soldiers riding out of formation. When they came up they explained that they were from Sweetwater station and would accompany us out of the trouble zone.

Before we started back the officer in charge spied a Colt's army revolver on one of the Missouri girls' self-appointed protectors and proceeded to relieve him of it, explaining that Colt's United States revolvers were regarded as government property and were not supposed to be carried by civilians.

As he handed over his gun, the young fellow got a mocking glance from the girls. His companion and two or three others suddenly remembered that they had urgent business down below.

The soldiers ate dinner near our camp and did not leave us for long during the remainder of the day.

The next day our party pulled out from the big train, glad to be to ourselves again. That afternoon the soldiers left us.

In the light of later events we may regard the clashes between the whites and the indians in the region recently traversed as the beginning of a series of engagements marking the progress in the conflict between the races due to the steady encroachment of the whites upon what the indians considered their rightful hunting grounds. To the former, westward migration meant homes and gold; to the latter, it meant the swift disappearance of the vast herds of buffalo and other wild game and with it, racial extinction. Elsewhere in this narrative I shall take occasion to pay tribute to the sterling qualities of the indian character as I know it through long years of association with various tribes. Here I shall merely say that though he could be a stanch friend, the red man, when the safety of his people was threatened, could also be an implacable foe. In *The Bozeman Trail* (Hebard and Brininstool) we read: "The beginning of the contest for territorial possession was in the raids by the indians; the results were the Platte Bridge fight, the Powder river indian expedition, the Fetterman disaster, and the Wagon Box and Hayfield fights. The finale was Custer's battle of the Little Big Horn."

Dog Travois

On the whole it is a record of treaties hastily entered into and lightly regarded, of misunderstanding on both sides and mistaken government policy. Yet here were the emigrants, subjected to increasing danger as a result of conditions beyond their control, their only protection the few soldiers that could be spared from the battlefront and their own rifles. Small wonder, then, that we were "all keyed up," as Mr. Ridgley put it. And we were thankful to be gradually leaving the region occupied by the Sioux and their allies, the Cheyennes and Arapahoes.

Chapter VIII
First Aid to the Injured

First Aid to the Injured

Another half day's travel brought us opposite Devil's gap. This is a great rift in the rocky wall where the Sweetwater, bending northward, breaks through the range of mountains of the same name. Our course was generally westward up the valley of the Sweetwater nearly to its source. During the afternoon we passed the carcasses of many animals, mostly cattle. The stench became more nauseating as we advanced. Why they had perished here in such numbers we could only conjecture. The day was sultry and a cloud of fine dust enveloped us. Our throats were parched with it. The oxen were restless and wanted water. At an early hour we turned out, having selected a place as free from the odor of carcasses as possible. The oxen, relieved of their yokes, started for water ahead of us. Most of them drank deeply from some standing pools before we could get them hazed on down to the river. Feed was good and we left them grazing quietly. As I recall, we did not put out any guards that night, feeling certain that the cattle would not stray far. Wearied with the day's journey, we retired early.

Next morning when I went out to look for the cattle, there lay Jerry, my off wheel ox, stark. He would never carry a yoke again. Red Tom, one of Dad Ridgley's leaders, was just able to rise. The others, including the two cows, were in a bad way. We thought that it must have been the stagnant water. Like most tenderfeet we knew nothing of alkali or its effects upon stock.

Something had to be done, and done quickly. What to do was the question. We had brought no stock remedies with us. As we watched the poor creatures writhing in their misery, we were confronted with the possibility that all of them might lay their bones among the skeletons by the wayside, leaving us stranded out in these wilds.

Of the many suggestions offered one at least seemed feasible, and that was to give them bacon. Some one remembered hearing that it had been tried under similar circumstances and found effective. So bacon it should be. We reached into our load and brought out slabs of the bacon which we cut into strips and proceeded to administer. Every "critter" rebelled. We coaxed and patted them. Still they remained obdurate. Finally, when all attempts at moral suasion failed, we felt that we must resort to methods of forcible feeding. Snubbing them up to the wagon wheels, we propped their mouths open and poked the slices of fat meat down with sticks, while the animals reared back, twisted, bucked and bawled simultaneously. Mrs. Ridgley thought it was a shame to pester the poor things that way. The rest of us had mixed feelings about it by that time. But we managed to get about two pounds down each one and there was plenty to spare, not including what went outside.

We waited awhile to note the effect of our heroic treatment. They seemed to be holding their own. We then yoked up, putting the two milch cows in place of Jerry and Tom (who was too weak to work) and started out.

It was a slow procession that made its way up the Sweetwater that day. The oxen staggered a little at times and needed to be eased along; but when night came again they were noticeably stronger than when we set out that forenoon. Our remedy had worked.

Sometime during the next day we met two mountain men who had their camp up in a draw north of the road. They made a business of buying alkalied or sore-footed stock and doctoring them up to sell again when cured. They also kept wild meat for sale. Dressed in fringed buckskin, their hair worn long, they seemed as intimately a part of the life of the wilderness as their indian wives and half-breed children. A few years, and their type would disappear with the vanishing border.

We followed the Sweetwater valley for four or five days, crossing the stream several times. Before reaching South pass we climbed a long slope at the top of which were many prospect holes perhaps five or six feet deep, with solid ice at their bottoms. We were told that ice springs abounded in this region. Although it was but the latter part of July, a cold wind from the snow-clad mountains to the southwest swept the ridge, chilling us through. Some placer claims had been staked out a few miles north of here. This was the beginning of South Pass City, which soon became a busy mining center, numbering some ten thousand souls when the excitement was at its height.

A short, steep descent, a stretch of level, and we were toiling upward toward South pass. Onward, upward among the pines, whose giant branches were extended in gestures of bestowal. To the north, remote, a triad of mountain majesty, the grand tetons towered above the surrounding peaks. Thinly veiled in the haze of midsummer, they looked like shadow mountains. To me there is nothing that equals a mountain in sublimity – except the endless surge of waters upon a rugged shore. Upward amid the glory of sunlit crags and flower-strewn slopes, of aspen thickets and flashing brooks. "A little nearer heaven than some of us may ever be again," someone remarked half in jest. I was certain that even the cattle were sensible of their changed surroundings. Perhaps it was the prospect of better feed.

On the last day of July we were in the pass. Here the Rockies dip, forming a broad passage-way so imperceptible in its east and west slopings that, try as we might, we could not tell where the water parting between the Gulf and Pacific slopes lay.

The western descent was accomplished without mishap and two or three days later found us in the valley of the Big Sandy, which flows southward into Green river about half way to Fort Bridger. Here we would soon leave the main Overland trail and proceed northwestward by a cut-off recently constructed under the direction of General Lander. This road crossed the Bear river mountains and the upper branches of the Snake, joining the Salt Lake and Virginia City road some thirty miles east of Fort Hall, and cutting in half the distance by the Salt Lake route.

With the building of highways over the land, there is an awakened interest in old trails. Believing that the Lander trail deserves more than casual treatment, I take occasion to refer to a portion of our correspondence with Ira H. Butterfield, of East Lansing, Michigan, who traveled that road in 1861. Mr. Butterfield was at one time secretary of the State Board of Agriculture and secretary of the Michigan State Agricultural College; of which institution his son, Doctor Kenyon L. Butterfield, is now president. A large part of his life has been in connection with the state fair and live-stock organizations.

The people of California were just beginning to turn their attention to agriculture and there began a demand for pure-bred stock to replace the old Spanish stock. Mr. Butterfield was a member of a party who drove a herd of pure-bred stock (seventy Shorthorn and Devon cattle and six hundred Merino sheep) to California in 1861, for John D. Patterson, a relative, then of Westfield,

New York. Mr. Patterson had been dealing in
pure-bred stock in California, shipping them by
way of the Isthmus of Panama. Steamer freights
were very high and he conceived the idea of driving a large number overland.

The expedition started from Nebraska City,
whither the stock had been shipped from Wisconsin, proceeded by the Platte route and the Lander
trail, striking into the west portion of Hudspedsth's
cut-off and into the Salt Lake road. From the big
bend of the Humboldt river they crossed the Nevada desert and passed over the Sierras from
Honey Lake valley, reaching Sacramento with a
loss of but one-fourth of the sheep.

"Taken altogether," writes Mr. Butterfield, "I
think this was one of the most remarkable trains
that crossed the country up to 1870, and perhaps
no other just like it ever made the whole distance
from Wisconsin to Sacramento. We had no sickness on the route and I could endure almost any
hardship when I got through. It was a daring un-
dertaking and only a peaceable indian situation
made it possible."

From a point just east of South pass, the Lander
road left the old Emigrant road and crossed the
range farther north beyond the head of the Sweetwater. Our trail cut across from Big Sandy and
joined the Lander road on Piney creek, an upper
tributary of Green river across the desert, as shown
on the accompanying map. We followed what was
known as the New Worked road. An idea of that

THE LANDER TRAIL

From a recent photograph of a scene on the eastern approach to the continental divide

portion of the route which we missed may be gained from the entries in the Butterfield *Journal* here given.

DAILY JOURNAL OF TRIP OVER LANDER'S ROAD IN 1861

JULY 20. Leaving the Salt Lake road at South pass so-called, drove 12 miles to the Sweetwater and camped one mile below the stage station. Here the road to Salt Lake leaves the Sweetwater to go over South pass. We were to take a road called Lander's road. So named after Colonel Lander, U. S. A., who had laid out the road in command of a United States Troop and had made it passable for teams. The road passed farther north than the Salt Lake road and while it crossed the summit at a higher elevation, it ran nearer the sources of streams and good water and grass was much more abundant. It is 250 miles from here to Salt Lake City. Met here a Mormon outfit going to Independence Rock to gather crude alkali salts which was used as soda for cooking. Our cook used some of this as an experiment for making biscuit and it answered the purpose. I do not know if the Mormons refined it in any way for use or used it in its crude state.

There is a stage station and a blacksmith shop here, the latter very useful, as by this time the horses of emigrants needed new shoes. In our train we took along an assortment of horse shoes and learned to put them on ourselves.

The dividing ridge is about eight miles from here and the Salt Lake road goes over or through South pass, which seemed to be simply a level place over the ridge where a road was possible and is not a gap or canyon as might be inferred.

JULY 21. We lay over here for the day. The nights were cold at this elevation (about 6000 feet) and this night ice two inches thick formed.

MONDAY, July 22. Broke camp at 4 A. M. and drove seven miles on the new road to Longs creek. There were three or four emigrant trains just ahead of us on this road. Good mountain water and good grass.

(By emigrant trains is meant a number of single family outfits and wagons joined together for better protection. There were from five to a dozen of these units travelling together. Sometimes we saw one family or wagon only, but these looked rather lonely.)

TUESDAY, July 23. Drove 12 miles to the Sweetwater which was here but a small creek. Passed today what was said to be the highest elevation on the road, 8300 feet above sea level. Fine mountain scenery.

WEDNESDAY, July 24. Drove six miles in the forenoon to Antelope meadows on Poors creek, a beautiful valley. Saw one antelope. Wind river mountains in view. Seemed near-peaks probably 50 or more miles distant. Fremont's peak in plain sight, 13000 feet elevation. In the afternoon drove seven miles to Little Sandy creek. Crossed the dividing ridge, 8250 feet above sea level. The streams now run into the Salt Lake basin.

THURSDAY, July 25. Drove five miles in forenoon to the head of Big Sandy and near high mountains. Took a tramp two or three miles up the mountains which are rocky. Numerous streams coming down over rocks made a noise like a miniature Niagara. In the afternoon drove to crossing of Big Sandy over a ridge from which we could see mountains covered with snow.

FRIDAY, July 26. Drove in the morning eight miles to Grass Springs. This is on the border of the upper part of the Colorado or American desert. On the Salt Lake road it is 50 miles wide without water or grass. As we were told on this road the longest stretch is 18 miles without water, but the road is sandy and dusty. Soil barren and covered with a small growth of sage brush. In the afternoon drove seven miles and camped on the desert.

SATURDAY, July 27. Broke camp at 3 A. M. and drove eleven miles to East Fork of Green river, a very swift stream about 20 rods wide and three feet deep. We crossed in the afternoon, swimming the sheep. Several of the men stationed at intervals in the river to help the sheep and all got over. Mosquitoes very thick.

SUNDAY, July 28. Drove eleven miles to Green river. At 5 1-2 miles struck the river and followed up 5 1-2 miles farther to a ford. Road hilly and dusty.

MONDAY, July 29. Crossed Green river. It

took all the forenoon. We had to unload wagons and put the sheep in them to cross as the river was too deep and strong to risk swimming and we had to raise the wagon boxes up from the bolsters to keep our provisions from getting wet. It was the most difficult stream on the whole trip to cross. In the afternoon drove thirteen miles, but the road was rough and the stock very tired.

TUESDAY, July 30. Lay over on Bitter Root creek to let the stock rest from the hard drive of Monday. In the evening we saw signal fires on the mountains made by indians. These signal fires were used by indians to communicate between different lodges or camps. The fires are kindled with light stuff to burn briskly for a short time and soon die out. One light means that strangers are in the vicinity; two calls the indians together; and three that they may attack the trespassers. We saw but a single light and rested quietly.

WEDNESDAY, July 31. Started at 3 A. M. and drove ten miles to the North Fork of Piney creek and in the afternoon three miles farther to the Middle fork of the same stream. Thornton and myself had gone back to Bitter Root creek to find a calf, whose dam had died there, the calf going back to seek its dam. We found the calf and with some trouble caught it (as we were not expert with the lasso) and led it back. It was dark long before we reached the place of noon camp but we could follow the road. We crossed the creek and kept on to the next fork where we expected to find camp. It was now midnight and we had had nothing to eat since noon and our horses were tired. We expected that a light would be kept to help us to locate camp but could not see any. We called aloud but no answer. I suggested firing my revolver, but Thornton would not listen to that as we were in an indian country. We finally gave up finding camp, tied our horses and the calf to trees and waited until morning. In the morning when we found camp one of the men on guard admitted hearing us call, but claimed he was so afraid of indians that he dared not answer – well, he got what he deserved from Thornton and me.

Chokecherries were already ripe in the draws and wild plums were turning. Currants and gooseberries were plentiful. We decided that here was just the place for a lay-over. Next day, while the usual round of washing, baking, and general tinkering was going on at camp some of us youngsters went out and brought in loads of these wild fruits. The women folk speedily made up quantities of preserves and "jell," which, served with hot biscuits and store tea, were a symphony in eating.

On the morrow we would take the short cut which led to Lander's cut-off, heading across the flats towards the Bear river range some three or four days' drive. That evening, our work finished early, we sat around the camp fire, telling stories and watching the world go by.

Chapter IX
Notes on Overland Travel

Notes on Overland Travel

It might be of interest to digress here in order to make a few observations concerning overland travel at this period. From Platte Bridge station on through South pass to where Lander's cut-off intersected the main trail there was a heavy volume of emigration. As before stated, we were seldom out of sight of other parties. The border states furnished the bulk of the traffic, with Missouri in the lead. Indeed, here was where one heard Missourian "as she was spoke." It was not unusual to see a whole neighborhood or clan on wheels, eager to leave a region where their sympathies and allegiance were so divided. Southerners, yankees, and people from the Great Lakes region came in about equal numbers.

Besides the "movers" and a few who packed through, were many government freighting outfits supplying the posts along the way, and privately-owned outfits with goods for the mines and intervening points. Then there were others who intended starting up in business and had brought goods along with them.

Last, but not the least important, were the stagecoaches carrying passengers, mail, and gold. Practically all of the gold shipments at this time, however, were by way of Salt Lake and the South Platte route.

Most of the trailers, like ourselves, used ordinary wagons, though many of the Murphy type with high, flaring boxes were in evidence. As yet there were but few wagon factories, so that wagon making, even with primitive tools, was still important as a home craft. One of our own wagons was homemade. During the winter when work was slack, it was not an uncommon sight to see a man who was handy with tools, at work on his wagon. A good home-made wagon was often hard to tell from a "boughten" one. A member of the younger generation recently asked me to explain how they did it. Fearing that my memory might play me tricks, I immediately went into conference with my neighbor, Tom Davis, who knows wagons from "a to izzard." Together we visited a forgotten corner of our premises where sundry parts of old freight wagons repose in a tangle of wild clematis and morning-glories. The following attempt at a description of a common method is the result of our cogitations.

Hardwood timbers for axles, bolsters, and other heavy parts were hewn with a broadax and shaped with a drawing knife. Swamp oak was the toughest wood for the purpose. A coupling pole, flattened at one end, was bolted in between the front "ex" and sandboard, the other end set between the bolsters and hind "ex," frequently with no provision

Tom Davis, Overland Freighter

for lengthening. A pole for the tongue was split partway up from the butt end to where it was bound beforehand with an iron band or rawhide to prevent further splitting, and set in place, the riven halves wedged apart and fastened with a queen bolt to pieces attached to the axle. This would allow free play up and down. There were no front hounds such as are found in later makes; the hind hounds were about the same as used today.

Hubs were hewn from the block and dressed down into shape. For these *bois d' arc,* or osage orange-wood, was a favorite material. Holes were cut to admit the axles and put in the spokes, after which the iron bands and linings were fitted in place. Spokes were split off with a frow and shaped, then set into the hubs. Holes were bored in the fellies and they were set in place, six on the front wheels and seven on the rear. Tires of the desired size were then put on, and the wheels were ready for business.

In the linch-pin type the spindle, or "skein," was protected by heavy pieces of strap-iron mortised into each side above and below, with iron rings at the shoulder and around the tip. The linch pin, which was flat, was dropped through a groove in the outer rim of the hub into a rectangular hole in the skein, and the wheel thus kept in place. The turning of the wheel prevented the pin from working out.

In making the box, crosspieces for the frame were selected, varying from thirty-eight inches in length for narrow tread to about forty-two inches for wide tread. Plank for the bottom, hewn or "whipped out" with a whipsaw, were laid upon these cross-pieces. Sides and ends, probably four feet high, with a flare of at least twenty inches, were placed upon this frame and supported at intervals by upright stakes set outside. As before stated, a straight or a flaring box came to be a matter of choice. Parts were all mortised together, no nails being used. A seat consisting of a board laid across two upright pieces might be put on when driving two or four animals with lines. There was sometimes a brake with a long rod and rope within easy reach of the driver if he rode his wheel mule. Practically all wagons, however, carried chains for rough-locking the wheels.

The whole was surmounted by a canvas cover supported by bows which widened outward if the box was flaring. To complete the picture, an oaken tarbucket hung at the rear, like the superfluous third party when "two's company, three's a crowd."

At the posts were usually men who broke in the mules for government work. People generally broke their own oxen. In breaking oxen, size and mating qualities were considered. A wild animal once broken in often proved more reliable than one which had been kept around the barn lot. To break one, "first catch your ox." Then snub him up to a wagon wheel or something solid and yoke him in with a well-broken ox. Put them in the center or "swing" and let them go with the load. If the new ox tries to twist around and get his head under the yoke, tie his tail to a chain. They learn it all in a little while.

In breaking two at a time they are sometimes yoked together and put behind another yoke of "broke" oxen, then driven around without the wagon for a while. Leaving a green pair yoked together over night often helps to gentle them. In rare cases a refractory animal may require special handling.

When yoking up we would drive the bunch into the circle if we corraled or alongside our wagon otherwise. Then we would take out a bow and put the yoke on the off wheeler, fastening the bow in with a key. The key was a triangular piece of wood which just fitted the hole in the end of the bow above where it went through the yoke, and was so notched that it could be turned sideways when in place and would not work out. Often more than one hole was cut in the bow for adjusting to different sized animals. Next we called up the other ox; or if he was slow about coming we let the end of the yoke rest on the ground while we got him. When yoked they usually went to their places of their own accord and the end of the tongue was put through the ring in the yoke. The others yoked and in place, we laid out the chains. One was fastened to the front "ex" or by a bolt to the tongue, then brought forward and hooked into the ring staple of the wheel yoke; another began here and hooked into the staple of the center yoke; and a third went from the ring of the center yoke to the staple of the lead yoke.

The driver walked on the left or "nigh" side and controlled his team with a crack of his whip and "Gee!" for the right, "Haw!" for the left, etc., with variations. The best drivers were invariably considerate of their animals. Your callous bullwhacker who cut the blood from their backs to display his skill usually had very little skill to display.

It is a picture that is fading – those old bull trains with their swaying canvas and rumbling wheels. Stalwart drivers urging their patient beasts with a crack of whip like pistol shots and an "Oop – hey, hey – ha, ha!" "Oh-ho-haw!" or "Ida-ho-ho, ho-ho, ho!" Merry childhood, rollicking youth, sober maturity, placid age. Faces turned westward, alight with hope, animated by high courage. Passing faces!

But I must not neglect the lowly mule and his part in the scheme of things. Great Murphy wagons, piled five or six feet high with freight for Fort Bridger, Salt Lake, or the mines, would pass us on the way, usually drawn by five-span mule-teams. The driver was a jaunty figure astride his nigh wheeler, the "jerkline" in one hand, a whip in the other. The "jerkline" was fastened to the nigh lead-mule's bridle and ran back through a ring in the left hame of each nigh mule. A "jockey-stick" reached from the nigh leader's hame to his mate's bridle for control, and the wheelers were connected by a "rum-strap" similarly fastened.

OVERLAND STAGE COACH OF THE SIXTIES

When the driver wished his team to swing to the left he would give the line a steady pull and call out "Haw!" To swing to the right he would give the line two or three short jerks and call "Gee!" Thus the nigh leader carried much of the responsibility for the behavior of the team. If some boneheaded mule displayed characteristic traits, the muleskinner was very expert with his long lash and the special vocabulary that grew up around the business of muleskinning.

Usually the mules grew so accustomed to the controls that, no matter how many span there were to the team, they would pull together as one; usually – but not always! Accidents *would* happen with the best regulated mule-teams, as for example when, on a frosty morning, a man's team would start "jack-knifing" on him.

Occasionally a trailer was put on, in which case eight or nine span were generally used. Later, on the Pierre trail, I frequently saw a cook-wagon behind the trailer, with ten or twelve span drawing the three wagons. The animals always matched in color and tapered in size from wheelers to leaders. It was an interesting sight when one of these outfits went prancing by with chain tugs jingling and metal on the harness gleaming in the sunlight. Occasionally men skilled in handling mules or oxen would while away an idle hour in friendly rivalry to determine who could drive closest to a given line without touching it or turn the "squarest" corner.

Following our camp on the Big Sandy we took the cut-off and were on our way across the level stretches in the direction of the Bear river range. There were eighteen or twenty wagons, including the Boutons, who were still with us. Just common folks, all of us – the kind that God must have loved, as our president once said, or He wouldn't have made so many of us.

A little better than halfway across we camped for the night on east fork of Green river. As I was taking the oxen out to feed I came across two graves in the midst of a thicket of boxelder. They were marked with stakes cut from the native wood. I looked for inscriptions, but if there had been any, time had obliterated them. From one of the graves grew a tree apparently at least twenty years old. I wondered if fur-traders hastening to the great rendezvous on Green river had placed their stricken comrades here. Possibly they were Mormons in search of a home in the wilderness.

Red Tom never recovered from the effects of the alkali. We led him behind one of the wagons, but he grew so lame Mr. Ridgley thought it would be useless to try to take him further. Before reaching the mountains we camped near a large village of Bannacks. Their chief came over to see us and to him Mr. Ridgley gave the ox, first assuring the indian that he hadn't got any "medicine" (poison).

The next day we camped at the foothills on a little stream known as Smith's Fork of Bear river.

Chapter X
A Diversion

A Diversion

As we entered the foot-hills of the Bear river range, our trail led up through a narrow canyon whose rocky walls rose sheer on either side of the shallow stream which flowed at its bottom. We were obliged to follow the bed of the stream for the most part, and as we urged our reluctant oxen along the uneven way, made doubly difficult by the adverse current over the slippery stones, our voices and the jolting of the wagons awoke a thousand echoes among the rocks.

Nor were we the only ones who found rough going; for presently on rounding a curve we began to distinguish the Oh! Ho! Haw! of trailers ahead. We seemed to be gaining upon them, for their language became increasingly more varied and colorful. "What kind of an outfit do you reckon that is?" I asked of Dad Ridgley, who was just ahead.

"Missourians," was the prompt rejoinder. "You kin tell a Missouri bull-whacker as fur as you kin hear 'im."

Missourians, it seemed, were unusually fertile in oral persuasion.

After some hours of this tedious travel, the canyon terminated abruptly and we entered a mountain glade, or park, where two creeks united to form the stream whose course we had been following. On a gentle rise just above the forks stood a blacksmith shop now fallen into disuse which was all that remained of a large government camp established a couple of years previously when Lander's cut-off was under construction. This was the first building of any sort I had seen since we left the indian cabins on the Pawnee reserve two months earlier.

The party who preceded us had corraled a little way from the blacksmith shop, and upon our approach the train captain urged us to make camp near them. Although it was still early we were not slow in accepting the invitation, as our cattle were footsore and needed a rest, and we ourselves were beginning to feel the effects of our strenuous trip through the canyon. Selecting a site near by we corraled and unyoked, after which Lon and I took the cattle up the north branch and left them feeding contentedly.

We now had an opportunity of becoming better acquainted with our new neighbors; for with the usual lack of ceremony characteristic of trailers in those days, visitors from the other camp were already arriving on the chance of seeing some one they knew or of hearing news from "back home." Theirs was an uncommonly large train – forty-five or fifty wagons in all. Missourians were in the majority, proving Dad Ridgley's surmise correct in the main, and all, with the exception of one small alien group, represented that restless border class who, for political and various other reasons, helped to swell the tide of westward migration during this period. A subtle difference, not easy to explain, characterized the little group of men and women who formed the exception. In dress, in manner, in personality, they seemed strangely at variance with their surroundings. "Town dudes" we called them for want of a more adequate term. We were soon to learn that they were a troupe of play folk from Chicago on their way to the mining camps, where their talent would insure them an eager welcome. The thirst for excitement and adventure; relief from conditions and obligations which the war had imposed; the lure of newly discovered gold in what is now southwestern Montana; an opportunity to secure free land in the fertile valleys adjacent to the mining camps — these factors accounted in a great measure for the motley character of the crowd. There were those who would live by their labor and those who would live by their wits.

The approach of supper time divided us into two camps once more. After supper we all met in the larger corral to talk over plans for resuming the journey from here. Our guide book stated that the distance across the range was about sixty miles, that the roads were very rough and rocky, and that feed was scarce. It was therefore urged that a day's rest would put the cattle in better condition for the trip across.

"Besides," added one, "there's no knowing how

long we'll be together after we get across, so let's make the most of it while we can."

And another, "I saw fish jumping up on all sides when I went for water."

This was a clincher, and we voted unanimously to lay over the next day.

When we got back Mrs. Ridgley began preparations for washing on the morrow, observing, as she put the clothes to soak, that the soft mountain water would lighten the work. We had been using alkali water most of the time since leaving the Platte. She also set some "salt rising."

Sunup next morning found most of us astir and eager to try our luck fishing. After a hasty breakfast, Dad Ridgley, Lon, and I got out our fishing tackle – without which no camp equipment was complete – and followed the north branch up to where the cattle were grazing. After noting that everything was all right with them, we caught some grasshoppers, baited our hooks, and started in. I was unused to fishing in rapid water and made a bad beginning. For one thing, I failed to remove the float and soon got my line tangled in the overhanging bushes. After several trials I managed to land one little fellow. "What luck are you having?" I then asked of Lon who had crossed the stream on a fallen log and was fishing a little farther down.

"I almost had one, but he flopped back in. He was sure a dandy," Lon answered ruefully.

We moved on down to where Dad Ridgley was hauling in one after another.

"Better take off your corks and part of your lead," he advised. This done he showed us how to cast, and we soon began to fare better. We fished on down to camp, cleaned our fish, and took them to Mrs. Ridgley. I had caught half a dozen medium sized ones and felt quite elated over my success. They were the first trout I had ever seen.

Lon and I then helped Mrs. Ridgley until dinner, our appetites sharpened by the tantalizing odors of frying fish. She set out choke-cherry "butter" and plum jelly which she had made during a day's layover on the Sweetwater, where these wild fruits grew in abundance. Then she opened tomatoes of her own canning. Our supply of potatoes having run out over a month earlier, a steaming bowl of hominy filled their place. Followed a loaf of the freshly baked "salt rising," then the crowning dish of all—a heaping platter of trout done to a turn. With fragrant coffee and real cream and brown sugar—the best we had in those days—here was a meal fit for a king.

"We haven't got much for dinner," remarked Mrs. Ridgley as she summoned us all to our places; "but as Aunt Evaline used to say, 'Eat Welcome, you're hearty.'" We needed no second bidding.

Scarcely were we through dinner when the captain of the other train, accompanied by a couple of the "town dudes," approached and wanted to know what luck we'd had.

"Tolerable," replied Dad Ridgley, indicating the fish bones piled up on our plates. "A body wouldn't need to be afeared o'starving to death if he was marooned up here, least ways as long as his fishing tackle held out."

"And the salt," supplemented Mrs. Ridgley.

"I reckon that's about right," returned the train captain. "Pears like everybody ketched about all they wanted. An' now that we've all took on a good feed and have a little time to kill, these here two fellers has got a proposition to make that'll put on the finishin' touches."

Whereupon one of the young men explained their "proposition" in this wise: "The last few days have been pretty tedious, and we've got a hard trip ahead of us. Only a few days longer and many of us will be going separate ways, most likely. So we've been talking it over among ourselves and we've decided to put on a little show this evening to liven things up a bit while we're all together. Your corral is smaller than ours and more conveniently situated for our purposes, and we'd like to know if you'll allow us to use it."

Would we? Dad Ridgley could hardly wait for him to put his request. "Come right along; an' anything we kin do to help out, jest let us know."

"Oh my!" chimed in Mrs. Ridgley, rising, "we'd love to have you." And for a moment she was silent. Even we boys with the elastic temperament of early youth, realized how the long days of monotonous travel in the heat and the dust, added to the ever-present fear of indian attack, had told on this courageous little woman.

"Then we'll begin preparations right away," the other young man hastened to add; and the three left us.

Soon all was bustle in the two corrals. Camp equipment in our corral was put in the wagons or shoved underneath so as to leave the enclosed space clear. Logs were cut in convenient lengths and placed in the "pit" forward of the entrance for the audience to sit upon. Meanwhile a "stage" was in process of construction out of materials at hand. A platform was built of loose boards from the blacksmith shop laid upon supporting timbers. Sheets salvaged from somebody's store of linen and strung on wires served for curtains; blankets hung at the sides and rear of the "stage," made effective interior walls. A square of "boughten" carpet; a couch improvised from a cedar chest, with pillows and drape; an engraving or two; a table with a lamp upon it, and two or three easy chairs conveniently placed – these completed the interior. A dressing room, also of blankets, was provided at each side. By this time a great quantity of dry wood had been piled at one side of the corral for lighting purposes, when all was in readiness. Everybody now dispersed for an early supper. As Dad Ridgley was getting down the grub box word came from the other corral that we were to go over and eat a snack with them. This relieved us from getting supper under difficulties.

Supper over, we were soon back at the wagons. While the men were shaving, Mrs. Ridgley laid out her one best dress – a figured bombazine with the flowing sleeves, short waist, and full skirt of that period. Presently she called to Dad Ridgley to come help her with the fastenings. As for Lon and me, our toilet preparations were simple enough. A trip to the creek where we scrubbed hands and faces till they tingled, then a perfunctory brushing of hair that would not stay put, and we were ready.

A faint glow tinged the western sky as we made our way down the aisle and selected a log well forward. A few had preceded us and were conversing in subdued tones as though under the spell of the hour and place. The seats began rapidly to fill. A small blaze gradually crept up through the pile of dead timber, diffusing a mellow light over all and casting grotesque shadows on the snowy canvas of the covered wagons opposite. Just without the circle of wagons, a group of somber spruces, ranged symmetrically like the columns of a mighty organ, caught the low tones of the evening wind and mingled them with the distant plash of falling water and the occasional call of a night bird. Darkly now the jagged mountain crests were outlined against the fathomless blue of the star-studded sky.

When the audience, numbering two hundred or more, were all seated, the orchestra began to make itself heard. From violin and flute, supported by the mellow chords of guitars, were evoked harmonies which sent our thoughts racing far away. Forgotten were the hardships of our journey, forgotten were its dangers. Our corral was a corral no longer, but a finely appointed theatre, and we ourselves an eager first night audience.

The music ceased abruptly and the curtains parted for the opening scene of a short play in which a young girl, who was about to be forced by mercenary parents into a marriage that was hateful to her, succeeded with the help of her sweetheart in disclosing some embarrassing situations in the elderly suitor's past, and thereby won the desired parental approval together with the final blessings.

During the applause which followed, I saw Mrs. Ridgley furtively wiping her eyes.

The next feature was a series of acrobatic stunts, at the conclusion of which the heavier of the two men who were performing stood on all fours while his lighter companion danced a jig on his back. Lon and I slipped over to one of the wagons and perched ourselves on a couple of wheels in order to get an unobstructed view.

A ventriloquist now convulsed his audience by mimicking cat and dog fights, Irish and negro dialect, familiar sounds from the farm, etc., besides making various persons say things they hadn't intended.

Popular song and instrumental numbers were rendered at appropriate places throughout the program. In addition to these, a chorus from one of the masters revealed the fact that here in this wilderness were assembled artists of no mean order of talent.

A group of old songs concluded the evening's entertainment. And as we took our way to our wagons in the soft light of the glowing embers, the melodies lingered with us after the voices and musical instruments were stilled.

We were climbing into our wagons for the night, our thoughts still afar on the wings of fancy, when suddenly the stillness was broken by the shrill staccato of a coyote. Lured by the firelight, yet wary as wild things are, the animal had waited until the fire burned low in the empty corral, when, yielding caution to curiosity, it had ventured quite near with its eerie challenge. A little way below at the head of the canyon its mate took up the cry. Cliff and crag multiplied the sound until the air was filled with the weird tumult. A moment it lasted. When the reluctant echoes died away, the spell was broken and we were brought back sharply to realities. It was not ours to ponder on the things we had forsaken at the beginning. Tomorrow was but a few hours away, and with it the stern demands of the trail.

Chapter XI
The End of the Trail

The End of the Trail

The following morning our party took the trail in advance of the other train. It was a "rocky road to Dublin" that we were to travel the next four or five days after leaving the friendly mountain park and its happy associations. When we struck the ridge there was scarcely a vestige of feed along the way except a little bunch-grass. If it hadn't been for the dwarf willows in the low places for the oxen to browse on they would have fared pretty slim. As it was we soon had to begin giving them rations of flour, using up two hundred pounds before we got across. There was heavy timber most of the way.

The second day we came to a steep hill and stopped to discuss plans for getting down safely. Some advised snubbing down with ropes, using trees for snubbing posts. Others thought it would be better to double-roughlock and let the two forward yoke of oxen follow each wagon and hold back by a chain reaching from the hind "ex" to their yokes, with the wheelers to guide the load. Two Cornishmen started down with only the rough-locks on, in spite of our protests. One side or the other of their wagons seemed to be in the air most of the time. No one else wished to imitate them. The heavily loaded wagons were snubbed down; the others, after double-rough-locking, we eased down with the oxen. All reached the bottom without serious mishap, and we were ready for the next adventure.

It came the following day. Black Tom, my nigh wheeler, had been displaying bovine traits. Usually so tractable, he seemed all at once to have developed a shut-in personality. In spite of all my prodding and vocal effort, as well as the example of the others of his kind, he simply went his own gait regardless. We were rounding a curve, the mountain wall at my right, a precipice yawning at my left. I holloed gee and the rest pulled up to the right; Tom went haw. The wagon started to slew, one wheel touching the edge. Another moment and we would be rolling down the canyon side to eternity. I stopped the oxen as quickly as I could and by that time half a dozen fellows had rushed over and were holding on to the upper side of the load to keep it from tipping. In a few minutes we had things righted and were on our way again.

The western descent was steep and rather sidling. We took the precaution to fasten a pole on the upper side of each wagon in such a way that one or two men could steady the load over the worst part.

Considering the limited amount of money that could be expended for road building and maintenance at that time, the road across this rough country was in very good condition. Fallen trees and loose rock had been cleared away and there were no bad ruts.

At last through the timber we caught glimpses of a beautiful green valley watered by a clear mountain stream. As we drew out into the open and consulted our guidebook we were not surprised to learn that we were in Paradise valley. (The name has since been changed to Star valley.) We followed the stream (Salt river) in its downward course three or four miles and crossed near where a small creek flowed in from the west. Here we camped for the night. Along the creek I noticed that the ground was encrusted with a white substance which I at first mistook for alkali. Tasting it, I found it to be salt, apparently in the pure state. This was a welcome discovery, and I gathered a heaping milkpan full to replenish our depleted stock. I also found the creek to be quite salt, although the larger stream bore no trace of it above here.

We were still in Wyoming, but were gradually approaching the Idaho line. Territorial boundaries were in process of being changed, and for some weeks after setting out on our journey, like the darkey in a late popular song, we didn't know where we were going, but we were on our way. The president had signed the bill on May 26, setting Montana apart from Idaho as a territory. When the news of this reached us I do not recall Yet so slowly did the doings of congress filter through, the watchword of many of our fellow travelers bound for Virginia City still was "Idaho."

We laid over a day in Paradise valley, enjoying
to the full the beauties of our surroundings. Game
was not so scarce here as along the main trails. One
of the men brought in an antelope and Lon got
some sage chickens. Our last fresh meat which we
had purchased from the mountain men on the
Sweetwater had given out some days before. There
were plenty of fish in the stream and wild fruits
along the banks, including a few service berries
that had not dried up yet. These somewhat resemb-
led the June berries at home and were good eaten
raw with cream and sugar, or in pies.

We left Salt river by a western branch of the
stream, crossed the Idaho line, passed Grey's Lake,
then drove northwest across Black Foot creek and
into the Snake river valley. I remember Black
Foot creek particularly on account of the fine
string of fish we caught.

It was along here that we beheld the daily mir-
acle of a desert sunset. Earth and sky merged in
perfect gradations of color and light from the
deepening purple of the far-flung plain to the softly luminous pearl-tints of the afterglow. And always the blue mountains in the distance rising in
solemn grandeur.

About thirty miles east of Fort Hall we joined
the Salt Lake and Virginia City road and were on
the main line of travel again. Soon we came to
another parting of the ways, where the Oregon
trail branched off by way of Fort Hall. Here we
parted with the Boutons, who took the westward

route and we continued northward to Morgan and Lowe's ferry.

At the ferry was a substantial frame house – the first dwelling we had seen since leaving the Pawnee settlement about two months earlier – which, together with bunk houses, stables and other buildings, served as a tavern and stage station also.

We took off all the oxen but the wheelers, removed their yokes and hazed them into the river. The current carried them downstream some distance before they reached the other shore. When they landed they shook themselves and began to browse as though nothing unusual had happened. We then drove upon the rope ferry and were carried across, two wagons at a time. It was getting on towards noon, but feed was scarce and we drove up the river eight or ten miles, turning out about four o'clock. Our road now led away from the river across a flat a good two days' drive to the hills beyond. They told us at the ferry that there was little chance of our finding water on the way across and that the roads were sandy and hard to travel. However, we might expect to find good feed around some outcroppings of sandrock a little better than halfway over. We therefore decided to lay over until mid-afternoon of the next day, fill our kegs and canteens with water in case we should have to make a dry camp, and drive at night on account of the heat.

The next forenoon I strolled up the river with my fish pole. Hardly had I thrown my hook in when a fish grabbed it and broke my line. I went back to camp for stronger line and when I returned to the river, I saw a man pulling out one fish after another. He didn't seem to be very cordial about my fishing there, so I moved down a piece and soon had a good string. By that time they had stopped biting where my neighbor was and he came on down. I told him to fish where I was, there was plenty of room. He did so, and when we had got what we wanted we counted sixteen apiece, all native trout. He caught the largest, which weighed two pounds and three quarters; but my string averaged a little better than his.

Late that afternoon we started across the flat. It was more pleasant traveling than in the heat of mid-day. About eleven o'clock the moon was hidden by a heavy bank of clouds. We urged the oxen forward hoping to reach our camping place before it should storm. Suddenly a wheel came off from the deacon's wagon, letting one corner down with a jolt. By the time the bur was hunted up and the wheel back in place ominous drops began to patter down upon the wagon covers. We pulled on a little further, then turned out just as the storm broke. We made short work of unyoking and hurried to cover while "the thunder rolled and the lightning flashed." Our camp was far from a dry one.

The next forenoon, after sleeping late, we yoked up and reached the desired camping place in the course of an hour. Not only was the feed excellent, but in the hollows of some flat rocks which covered a small plateau we found that water had collected more than sufficient for our needs. Here we laid over till the next morning, reaching the hills late that afternoon.

Just as we were starting out on the following morning we saw eight or ten men riding along the road toward us. After a short conference with their spokesman Mr. Ridgley accompanied them a little distance away, returning in a few minutes and we drove on. Not until noon did he satisfy our curiosity. Then he explained that these men were Vigilantes hastening to the scene of the Portneuf creek raid upon the Overland stage, in which road agents robbed the coach of a heavy gold shipment a few days earlier. Some of the Vigilantes were Masons. Mr. Ridgley's being a Mason also probably led them to speak more freely with him of their mission.

One evening we pulled in with some freighters from Salt Lake with potatoes for the mines. They were out of flour. We were out of potatoes. They offered to trade us pound for pound and we gladly let them have fifty pounds of flour in exchange for an equal amount of potatoes. They told us they received twenty-eight cents a pound gold price or fifty-six cents greenbacks for potatoes.

Stage-coaches passed us frequently and we sometimes caught fleeting glimpses of passengers within. The old Concord coach was a handsome equipage as it rolled along behind its six prancing horses. The body was slung on heavy leathers which great-

ly modified the jolting and allowed a gently swaying motion. The two seats within faced each other
and usually accommodated three average sized
persons apiece. There was a high seat in front for
the driver and a movable dashboard with an enclosed space beneath for parcels. At the back was
an extension called the "boot" where baggage was
carried. Light articles could be put on top as well.

Ben Holladay's stage line operated between
Saint Louis and Sacramento and the stages which
served the mines connected at Salt Lake. The trip
east could be made in something like seventeen
days of continuous travel. Ben Holladay's name
was as famous in passenger transportation as Rus-
sell, Majors and Waddell in carrying freight.

On the last day of August we were through the
pass. On the fifth of September we selected a camp
site on a flat a little way southwest of Virginia
City – our destination.

Chapter XII
Virginia City

Virginia City

For exactly four months we had been occupied in getting to Virginia City. Now that we had arrived we were in the same state of mind as the late American expeditionary forces when they began asking "Where do we go from here?" All of our fellow travelers except the deacon and Alonzo had scattered. We suddenly found ourselves confronted by entirely new sets of conditions and needed time to get our bearings.

We made our camp on a flat about a mile southwest of Virginia City where feed was plentiful, and from there we visited the various camps in Alder Gulch. There were four of the larger camps: Nevada, or Lower Town, Virginia City, Highland, and Summit, which, together with the smaller diggings, extended in the order given the whole length of Alder Gulch, a distance of about twenty miles.

The boom was on. Every foot of ground along the creek had been staked out and men were busy sluicing out the precious metal whose magic presence had drawn recruits from every class and locality. Each claim bordered the creek. The sluices were about a foot deep and fifteen to twenty inches wide. They were built in sections which tapered

slightly at the lower end so that they could be fitted
together for any length desired. They were placed
upon supports and pitched with reference to the
grade of the creek and the character of the dirt.
False bottoms, perforated and fitted with cross
slats, were set in the sluices to catch the gold. One
man stood at the upper end and shoveled in the
gravel, first stripping the surface down to pay dirt,
if necessary. Another threw out the rocks with a
steel fork, while a third shoveled away the tailings.
Only the gold and the heavy black sand remained.
Guards were left at night except in case of a daily
"clean-up." In cleaning up, the false bottoms were
raised and the deposit put in gold pans to be washed. When the black sand was removed the gold
was dried and put in buckskin bags. Blowers were
used to free the gold from remaining particles of
foreign substance when it was weighed out. These
blowers, which accompanied the gold scales, were
rectangular metal plates with edges turned up on
three sides. The particles of gold were blown from
one upon the other, the lighter foreign matter falling clear. Gold passed current at the rate of $18.00
an ounce, ninety cents a pennyweight, and three
and three-fourths cents a grain.

Of the four mining towns in the gulch, Virginia
City was destined to lead in importance. If we expected to see a sprawling town of shacks we were
doomed to disappointment. Instead, an orderly
village of neat log and frame buildings nestled in
a sheltered basin where a tiny stream, fed by a ser-

VIRGINIA CITY, MONTANA
As it appeared in 1864

ies of springs, reached Alder creek from the north through a tangle of alder and willow.

The streets were lined with bull-trains and pack-animals. From the farther diggings buckskin-clad miners, with beards and flowing hair, hiked in for supplies which they carried away in enormous packs strapped upon their backs. Strings of donkeys loaded with everything from groceries to lumber took the steep trails into the hills.

Merchants were busy at their counters or replenishing their stocks from the freight trains hurrying in from the south while the pass was still open to travel. As in every frontier town of that day places of amusement were running full blast. School facilities, religious services, banks and other business enterprises supplied the growing needs of a population already numbering upwards of five thousand. The terrtorial court convened here, and preparations were being made to move the capital over from Bannack. Much of the household labor was performed by Chinamen, who also conducted laundries and restaurants and worked in the mines.

This was no "Main Street town" like those to which we were accustomed back in the states, but a community where life was lived to the full. Yet so completely had the forces of law and order operated that there was little to suggest the reign of violence and disorder of a few months past.

Indeed, my hopes for a bit of gun-play were likely to be dashed but for the following incident, in which I was cast for a stellar part. It was near the close of our stay at the camp site near Virginia City. The cattle were grazing on a hillside below me. I had taken my shotgun along on the chance of seeing a grouse. Two horsemen rode over the brow of the hill, scaring up a jackrabbit as they approached. I saw the rabbit and cocked my gun in readiness to fire. The rabbit disappeared behind some sagebrush, and I rested the gun, stock downward, thumb on the hammer, waiting for it to show up. Thinking it might have followed a blind path through the sagebrush, I removed my thumb, when suddenly both barrels discharged in mid-air with a tremendous roar and a kick that sent a spasm of pain through my big toe where I had thoughtlessly rested the gun. The rabbit was horribly frightened and ran with a little screech past me.

"There he goes!" shouted one of the horsemen.

"Damn the rabbit!" I howled as I nursed my injured toe.

After looking things over and studying the situation carefully for nearly a fortnight, Dad Ridgley declared himself in this wise one evening:

"I kin handle a plow better'n I kin a gold pan."

Then he and the deacon fell to discussing glowing reports of a farming section newly opened to settlement on the Gallatin, sixty miles north. Bozeman himself had ridden on in advance of his party, located the townsite which was to bear his name, and was active in inducing immigrants to settle in this region. Loads of produce had already come in

from the East Gallatin where a small settlement
had sprung up the year before. These brought
good prices. The men believed that they could do
better to take up land and raise produce for the
mines than to try their luck here where the hazards
were so great.

And so it came about that on the seventeenth we
were passing through Virginia City on our way to
the Gallatin country. Meanwhile a scaffold was
being raised on the flat between Virginia City and
Nevada where, later in the day, another example
of the summary retribution of mountain law was
given to the world. A robber by the name of John
Dolan had been brought in the day before. He was
implicated in the Portneuf raid upon the stage-
coach mentioned in the preceding chapter. His
latest offense was relieving one James Brady of
$700 in gold. For these and other offenses he was
tried by the Vigilantes and executed in the presence
of a great crowd of witnesses. His pal, Jem Kelly,
also one of the participants in the raid on Portneuf
creek, had been apprehended by the party of Vigilantes whom we met on Snake river and hanged
near Fort Hall, we subsequently learned.

Until recently the road agents had dominated
the situation, when their power was effectually
broken through the agency of the Vigilantes acting
when civil law was as yet inoperative. A brief
summary of their activities as they were related to
us while at Virginia City might not be amiss here.

The discovery of gold in paying quantities by

John White at Bannack in 1862 was followed by an influx of gold seekers from all parts of the West. Among them were many from the lawless classes whose sole purpose in coming to the mines was to prey upon those who had made their stake by fair means.

Another rich find the following spring precipitated another stampede on a larger scale. During the latter part of May a small party of prospectors were returning to Bannack from the Jefferson, whither they had gone in a vain attempt to overtake a larger party of prospectors bound for the Yellowstone under the leadership of James Stuart. They were Bill Fairweather, Henry Edgar, Barney Hughes, Tom Cover and two others whose names I do not remember. They camped for dinner, May 26, on a small stream flowing into an upper branch of the Jefferson. While dinner was being prepared Fairweather asked a couple of his companions to go with him down the gulch to try their luck. The others argued that the gulch had been throughly prospected and it would be only time wasted. Fairweather then went down alone. When he didn't show up, they grew tired of waiting and ate their dinner. While the rest packed up Edgar went down after him. He didn't come back either. The four men remaining then followed to see what was up. There they found the two busily panning out the yellow metal. It didn't take long for them to get their gold pans and join them. After washing out a considerable sum they covered

FIRST CAPITOL BUILDING IN MONTANA
The tall building at the right as it appeared in Virginia City, 1864

up their traces and returned to Bannack for supplies. They tried to keep their discovery a secret, but the news leaked out somehow. The upshot of it was that when they went back to Alder Gulch, as they called it, most of Bannack went with them. During the rush that followed more than sixty thousand people gathered there and $100,000,000 in gold was taken out in the course of the next few years.

No sooner did the gold shipments begin than the road agents banded together and carried on an organized system of robberies and murders which threatened to outrival conditions during the California gold rush. They soon came under the leadership of Henry Plummer, himself a bold and desperate character from California. Plummer had great tact and executive ability, besides being a man of engaging presence and the best shot in the country. He was not long in getting himself elected sheriff of both Bannack and Virginia City. For his deputies he chose leading members of his band and thus, protected by the law, made himself master in a regime of crime. Among his deputies were Jack Gallagher, Buck Stinson, Ned Ray, and a man named Dillingham. Later George Lane, or Club Foot George, joined his forces and was most active in securing information about gold shipments and "planting" holdups. Red Yager was messenger and Brown corresponding secretary.

Stage coaches carrying treasure were mysteriously marked in a manner which enabled members of the gang to communicate with their confederates in time to prepare for the holdup in some lonely place. Occasionally a member of the gang would accompany the stage as a "guard" or even drive the outfit without being suspected, in order to facilitate matters. The robbers sprang from concealment with levelled guns, called out with their customary profanity, "Halt! Hands up!" and proceeded to relieve the coach and its occupants of their gold and valuables. Resistance meant almost certain death. This done, they were told to drive on and the outlaws rode away to divide up their haul.

This wholesale murder and rapine continued for over a year and a half, during which time no man's life or property was safe. They even murdered Dillingham, one of their own members, for warning a friend of an intended robbery. When the miners' courts were resorted to, juries were packed, judges were bought off and false witnesses were brought in. With one notable exception, a trial was merely a farce and conviction well nigh impossible.

Finally two murders occurring close together aroused the people to such a pitch that definite steps were taken to check the course of the road agents. The murdered men were Nicholas Tbalt and Lloyd Magruder.

Tbalt, a young ranch hand, was shot and robbed by George Ives on a ranch near Nevada. His body was concealed in the brush. A hunter shot a grouse

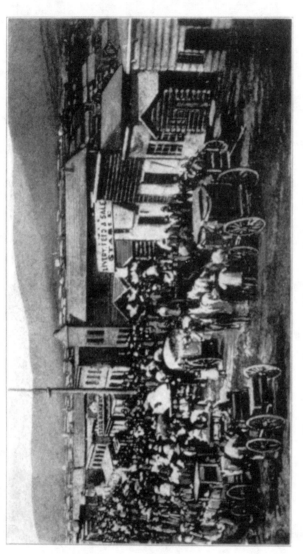

Fourth of July in Nevada, Alder Gulch, 1865

which fell upon the body of the murdered man
and thus led to a disclosure of the crime. Ives was
taken to Nevada by a posse of twenty-six men pled-
ged to stand together, and tried next day in the
miners' court by a jury of the people, Colonel W.
F. Sanders presiding. Ives's execution took place
within the hour of his conviction, December 21,
1863.

The murder of Magruder, a popular merchant,
and his four companions by Plummer's band was
the last determining factor in the formation of a
Vigilance committee. Magruder had brought over
a pack-train load of merchandise from Lewiston
to Virginia City, sold it out in the late summer and
was returning with four friends to Lewiston.
Hearing of this, Plummer sent four of his band to
join them. Under the guise of miners returning
to California these men offered their services to
Magruder in return for free transportation as far
as Lewiston. Magruder engaged them and supplied them with fresh mounts. In a mountain canyon beyond the Clearwater the robbers murdered
the five men and escaped with their loot.

They passed through Lewiston on their way to
California. Suspicion was aroused by their strange
behavior and Hill Beecher, the deputy marshal,
was sent after them. He followed them to California and brought them back to Lewiston single
handed on requisition of the governor of Idaho
territory. They were immediately tried and executed. The work of this intrepid officer is almost

without parallel, considering the fact that every possible obstacle was laid in his way while in the performance of his duty.

In December a small self-constituted band of men from Virginia City and Nevada quietly enlisted the interest of other men from the better classes and the formation of a Vigilance committee was quickly under way. They took the following "Vigilante Oath:"

> We, the undersigned, uniting ourselves in a party for the purpose of arresting thieves and murderers, and recovering stolen property, do pledge ourselves upon our sacred honor, each to all others, and solemnly swear that we will reveal no secrets, violate no laws of right, and not desert each other or our standards of justice. So help me God as witness our hand and seals this 23rd day of December, 1863.

Regularly organized and gaining rapidly in numbers, this secret tribunal pitted its strength against that of the road agents, likewise fully organized and working in secret.

By the end of January, 1864, they executed twenty-four of the robber band, including their wily leader, Henry Plummer, and banished or silenced the remainder. The confession of one of their number, Red Yager, had put them in possession of the names of the members. When their work was finished and the district was safe for her citizens, they quietly gave way to the civil law, standing by in case their services should be needed again.

As we toiled slowly up the ridge to the north, our parting glimpse of Virginia City included Cemetery Hill and the row of white stakes which marked the graves of the road agents who met their doom that fatal fourteenth of January.

Chapter XIII
The Passing of Custom

The Passing of Custom

Over rolling uplands, brown and parched, we traveled most of the day of our departure from Virginia City. The Bozeman and Bridger trains had pulled in close together about six weeks earlier. It struck me rather oddly to be following in reverse order the very trail that we had vainly hoped to have a part in blazing.

Toward evening our road descended abruptly into the valley of the Madison. Just before we reached Fores's Crossing we met two wagon loads of produce from the Gallatin valley. We bought some vegetables, including a big mess of turnips at six cents a pound. So hungry were we for turnips that we ate quite heartily of them at supper. Too heartily, I fear; for sometime in the wee sma' hours we paid our first visit to the medicine chest which we carried along for emergencies. Good old Doctor McArthur, whom we employed by the year, had taken great pains in filling the chest just before we started.

The water was low and we forded the river the next day. In wading across I struck my sore toe against a rock and in consequence had to spend some months growing a new toe-nail.

Another two days across an upland prairie be-

tween the Madison and Gallatin, and we were
nearing our journey's end. On the twentieth of September we looked across a broad expanse of valley
land, watered by tree-bordered streams which
flashed in the sunlight where they met out beyond
a great arc of snow-clad mountains. The most
beautiful spot in the world. Gallatin valley! Down
to the West Gallatin we drove and along its southern bank until we came to a lower crossing. This
was an ancient highway of the indians leading to
the great hunting region of the Yellowstone. Here
Chief Joseph of the Nez Percés, had passed eastward at the head of his band only a few days earlier. The hoof and travois marks of their caravan
were still fresh. We forded the river, continued
northward about two miles and camped near a
spring a half mile from the river.

"This is good enough," was the general ver-
dict. And here in this beauty spot our camp was
speedily transformed into the home that was to be.

Dad Ridgley staked off his quarter section from
the spring to the river; the deacon chose a piece
adjoining on the east; and Alonzo took a claim to
the east of his father's. All three claims paralleled
the river.

Having decided on the location for our buildings we unloaded the wagons, removed the boxes,
and reloaded them to serve as temporary shelter.
We spent the day sharpening axes, saws, and
scythes. While the men were cutting and hauling
in the cottonwood house logs, I took my scythe and

began cutting hay in the low places to the north
of us. I was not a little proud of my skill as the
lush bluestem and redtop, waist high, fell in neat
windrows at the swing of my scythe, later to be
bunched with a fork when cured. Aching muscles,
however, checked my enthusiasm until I grew accustomed to the extra exertion.

Before cold weather set in we were comfortably
settled in our new cabin. We had also built a stable
big enough for three milch cows and a team, with
room to spare for an extra saddle horse. We bought
a fresh milch cow and a light span of ponies from
a rancher down the river. Hay to last us through
the winter was stacked in a pole corral next to the
stable. A "cave" or root-cellar was shortly completed.

Along the stream were many clumps of buf-
alo-berry bushes. After the first frost we beat the
berries from the bushes upon canvas or blankets
and Mrs. Ridgley added buffalo-berry jam and
jelly to her store of preserved fruits.

Our cabin measured sixteen by twenty feet in the
clear. The logs were chinked and pointed with
clay. The roof was of poles covered with hay and
sodded; we filled in the crevices with loose dirt,
fondly hoping that it wouldn't leak. The floor was
of earth, beaten hard and smooth. Door and window frames were hewn from the timber and dressed down with a drawing-knife. The one door of
puncheons, fastened together with pins, swung on
wooden hinges, with the latch string "on the out-

side." We were quite vain of our two windows of glass with their ruffled white curtains. Most of our neighbors had to content themselves with oiled muslin to let in the light.

A corded bed with a patchwork coverlet stood against the west wall; my own trundle-bed was pushed underneath. At one side stood the chest of drawers with a braided rug in front. There were three split-bottomed chairs and a wash-stand of puncheon upon supporting pins. Our first table was of puncheons. Later we got boards for a new table from a couple of men up the river who were "whipping out" lumber for their own use. A box cupboard held our stock of dishes and cooking utensils. Beside it stood the churn. The flour barrel was converted into a "center-table" whereon reposed the family Bible and photograph album with their white lace covers. A box of seashells, a vase of feather flowers, a small mirror and a colored print or two added to the cheerfulness of the room. Not a nail had been used throughout the building; all parts had been pinned or mortised.

When the candles were lighted and the supper things cleared away, it was solid comfort to draw up around the fire and read or chat. The old clock with its heavy weights ticked against the wall, and Shep, dozing in his corner, would growl fitfully as though recalling some exciting experience of his early doghood. Let the storm rage outside; we were sheltered and safe from its rigors.

The deacon and Alonzo, snugly settled in their

cabins, were frequent visitors. Other settlers came in until by Thanksgiving we were quite a little community on the West Branch. Among the new arrivals were Mr. and Mrs. Charley Blakeley and their two children from the south, who moved in just below the crossing. Mrs. Ridgley declared, when she first met Mrs. Blakeley, that she'd just got plum lonesome for the sight of another woman.

Nearly a mile below us three young fellows from Missouri had put up a cabin. Their names were Bob Vivian, Dave Ballantyne and Vard Cockerell. They were shortly joined by a colored family from their home community – Old Uncle Harrison, his wife, Georgeanna, and their three children. These darkies knew many home crafts and were of the greatest assistance to their neighbors in opening up new farms. Their geniality and kindliness won them friends everywhere. The story of their earlier life and their coming to Montana interested us greatly, and I will tell it briefly as we heard it.

At his master's death Uncle Harrison was given his freedom. Not wishing to leave his mistress he stayed on and served her faithfully. In the course of time he met Georgeanna. He bought her with the savings of years and they were married. They lived with the old mistress until her death, when it was found that she had willed the plantation to them. Other heirs pressed their claims; the will was contested; and Uncle Harrison and his family were dispossessed and forced to leave, almost penniless. They joined an expedition for Virginia

City where they were eagerly welcomed by our bachelor friends and brought to the valley. They were duly installed in the cabin, where George-anna reigned supreme; and the men immediately set about building a new house close by for themselves.

It was now time to go and kill our winter's meat. We hitched up our newly-acquired team to a newly-acquired light wagon and with guns, ammunition, grub, and bedding set out for the mountains just north of the pass. A heavier wagon drawn by two yoke of oxen followed to bring back our kill. We camped at the Philipps boys' cabin, twenty miles up the East Branch. The boys were away at work and we didn't get to see them.

Game was so plentiful on the face of the mountains five or six miles farther that there was no difficulty in finding all we wanted. In a couple of days more we started back with elk and venison enough to last the deacon and Lon and ourselves till spring. We hung the meat up on the north side of our cabins out of reach of predatory animals, where it kept in good shape till we used it up.

There were antelope aplenty right around home. At first I used to count them as they bounded along the trail they had worn between us and the river — ten, fifteen, twenty in a band. After awhile the novelty wore off. They were shy creatures; but their curiosity often overcame their shyness, sometimes to their sorrow. Having left my jacket in the timber where we were cutting poles, I threw a blanket over my shoulders one snappy morning and started down to get it. On the way a bunch of antelope came in sight. I crouched with the blanket over my head until they all surrounded me, their eyes big with wonder. Jumping to my feet I waved my blanket at them and you should have seen them scatter!

North of our claim there was an open space or glade next to the swamp. Here wild artichokes grew in great abundance and here grizzly bears came in the night to harvest those same artichokes. And a thorough job they made of it, too. Of this I was convinced as I hurried across the furrowed ground to the hay lot. The folks laughed at my fears and I told them to come and see for themselves.

"Ef ye see a bar," Dad Ridgley advised, "look 'im square in the eye and he'll turn and run."

Nevertheless Mr. Ridgley shortly afterward took his muzzle-loading rifle and strolled down that way. He came back faster than he went. Briefly stated, his adventure runs as follows:

On rounding a clump of brush he had seen a grizzly "as big as Red Tom." The critter was standing upright, greedily stripping buffalo berries from the branches and eating them with audible enjoyment. Both were greatly surprised at the sudden encounter. Not wishing to push the acquaintance further, each turned and went his separate way. Dad Ridgley explained that if he had fired and failed to hit the bear in a vulnerable spot the first time, the animal might have been too quick for him.

On October 24, Governor Edgerton called the first territorial election to choose members for the legislature and a delegate to congress. At this combined election and settlers' meeting, affairs of common interest were discussed. Men were present who were familiar with customs and conditions in the mining and agricultural regions of Colorado, California and Oregon. With their help, by-laws were adopted covering all ordinary cases that might arise during the period that would elapse before territorial laws could be passed and become effective. We were assured that by-laws so passed would be sustained by the courts. This assurance was substantially borne out later, and the custom of a people , through legislative enactment, passed into law. Meanwhile, with the nearest seat of justice a thousand miles away, the people of the territory, through the miners' and settlers' meetings, remained supreme.

The growth and development of this section was typical of the change gradually taking place throughout the Northwest, where roving indian tribes, trappers, missionaries, and miners were for many years the only inhabitants. To Mrs. W. J. Beall, who still lives as the revered "Mother of Bozeman City," I am indebted for an account of the settlement prior to our coming.

Among the first settlers were A. K. Stanton, W. H. Tracy, F. F. Dunbar, D. E. Rouse and brother,

Elisha and W. D. P. Hayes. These men came into the valley in 1862-1863, locating old Gallatin City and taking up ranches in that vicinity and on East Gallatin and Reece creek. In July, 1864, Mr. Beall and Mr. Rouse, returning from a marketing trip to Virginia City, met John M. Bozeman riding in advance of the train which he was piloting from the East over Bozeman cut-off. Plans already under way for a townsite were concluded with Bozeman's request that Beall, Rouse, and W. W. Alderson stake off cornering claims, reserving one for him. This was done, and by August 9, the organization was perfected. Town lots were offered free as an inducement to build. A number from Bozeman's train stopped off. Other settlers followed until there were at the time of our arrival six or seven houses in Bozeman and as many in the vicinity.

It was a happy reunion when the Philipps boys, returning from work, stopped for the night at our place. When questioned about their trip over the Bozeman trail they told us that nothing more exciting than a stampede of the cattle had happened on the way.

"It was over in the Tongue river country next to the Big Horns," they said; "and it goes to show how even the gentlest animals will act when they're excited. We had just turned out one evening after a day of continual prodding and urging to get our cattle to move faster than a snail's pace. A herd of buffalo drifted down from the mountains and joined them; whereupon they all struck out across the prairie as though possessed. Some of the oxen, heads and tails in the air, were in the lead. They must have run twenty miles before Bozeman and the rest of the bunch could get them cut out and headed for camp."

When asked about indians they replied that twice roving bands had crept up within gunshot of their camp, but had left when they saw the sentinels watching them.

Virginia City was then our nearest post office. Whoever went in with produce usually took our letters and brought back the mail. Sometime in the fall Charley Smith, from down near the "Forks," began gathering letters over the valley and taking them in every other week. It took him about two weeks to make the rounds and his charge was twenty-five cents for each piece of mail. Letter postage was then about twenty-five cents per $\frac{1}{2}$ ounce so that at fifty cents each, letters were likely to be few and far between. A letter was generally so written that the sheet could be folded, sealed, and addressed for mailing. An envelope or an extra sheet, meant an additional charge at the same rate.

We began receiving copies of the *Montana Post,* and the arrival of this valuable weekly was an event in our neighborhood. The price of subscription was $5.00 per year at first and later $7.50. An idea of the purpose and aims of the periodical may be gained from the following excerpt under date of Saturday, August 27, 1864:

In presenting the first number of the *Montana Post* to our readers, it is but proper that we briefly lay down the principles that are to govern us as a journalist. In the first place our main object when we left our home to bring a press to the 'Far West' was to publish a journal devoted to the interest of the people now inhabiting, and who design to remove to this new, and soon to be most important, territory of the United States. The interest of the miner, the agriculturist, and the business man will be carefully looked after. We will have correspondents in the various mining camps, who will keep our readers well posted in all that is going on in the different parts of our young and rapidly growing territory.

(Market reports, literary essays and miscellaneous articles were to appear. No personalities were to be indulged in, the purpose of the journal being to pursue an independent and straightforward course. No political clique or faction should be favored. Being "in no man's hire," the interest of all alike would be considered and independent views on all national questions would be given.)

Relying, therefore, on the generous people for a present and future support, and making our kindest bow, we introduce ourselves.

It is noteworthy that this periodical more than fulfilled its promise and maintained the same high standard of journalism throughout its existence.

On one of his visits Jim Bridger told of a region at the head of the Yellowstone where hot water spouted from glistening craters with a tremendous roar. There were queer formations and strange noises. Some were inclined to think that it was just another of Bridger's yarns until parties went and saw for themselves this wonderland which came to be known as the Yellowstone National Park.

Bridger was then a government scout subject to call. He has undoubtedly been the most active figure in the winning of the Northwest. I occasionally meet other old timers whose memory of Bridger confirms our own in respect to his character, and who keenly resent any portrayal of the great scout in a trival fashion. A. D. Haworth, of Story, Wyoming, who was a life-long friend of Bridger, states emphatically that "he never consorted with indian women or caroused around."

F. W. Rich, of Dean, Montana, joins me in my endeavor to be of aid in keeping a true perpsective of this sturdy character. Mr. Rich crossed the plains in 1866 in a train of emigrants that was under command of Jim Bridger after leaving Fort Reno, on Powder river. He rode in the advance guard with Bridger the following three months until the train reached Bozeman and is a great admirer of Bridger both as a scout and as an individual. During his many years of acquaintance with the great plainsman he states that he never heard of his being drunk.

He describes Bridger as being "a stern, curt, typical frontiersman who took a drink of whiskey when and where he pleased, never to the detriment of his senses, and although he was cautious and was educated in indian ways, he knew no fear."

Winter closed in early that year. Aside from our regular chores we did little more than get out what poles we would need to inclose our field next spring. We depended almost entirely upon our paper for news of the outside world. When storms delayed the mails from the East there were always local matters of interest from the mining camps. The following item which appeared in a belated copy of the *Post* will serve to show that even out here questions of more than local interest were receiving attention:

A clergyman at an afternoon service was asked to read a notice for a woman's rights meeting, which he did in this wise, "At half past six o'clock in the school house, in the first district, a hen will attempt to crow."

Chapter XIV

A Caravan of the Wilderness

A Caravan of the Wilderness

One blustery forenoon, late in March, Dad Ridgley, responding to a knock at the door, admitted three men who were wintering in a cabin on the West Branch near the upper crossing. They were thin to emaciation as though the season had dealt unkindly with them.

"We heard you had some flour," their spokesman explained, "and we came to see if you would sell us a little. For three months we've been living on meat straight, and the last three weeks of that time, on meat without salt. You know what that will do to a fellow." And he smiled wryly.

"I kin let ye have fifty pounds," Dad Ridgley promptly told them. "We kin make out," he assured them, sensing their great need; and getting his steelyards he weighed it out for them.

When they wanted to know the price, he told them fifteen dollars.

"But don't you know what flour is selling for in Virginia City?" they asked. "Ninety dollars a hundred, and still going up. We will gladly pay you at that rate. We haven't been able to get it here at any price."

Dad Ridgley did know about prices in Virginia City since early storms had tied up traffic, but he answered: "I figger it's worth fifteen dollars, jest what I'd a had to pay when we landed, and that's what I'll charge ye."

Then from our meager supply of salt he let them have enough to tide them over.

Meanwhile Mrs. Ridgley set about preparing an early dinner, and in an incredibly short time a meal so appetizing that it fairly took your breath steamed upon the table. From the depths of her flour barrel, where were stored her supply of home-canned products from Wisconsin, she had brought out a tin of preserved pumpkin. Too plebeian to have a place on her list, it had gotten in by mistake; now, after many months, a dish of this same lowly pumpkin was to be the piece de resistance of our meal.

An hour or so later, when we sped them on their way, our visitors trudged homeward through the snow in the best of spirits, each taking his turn with the sack of flour.

This incident serves to illustrate conditions at this time. Owing to the enormous immigration, large supplies of provisions were ordered from Salt Lake, but early storms caught the freighters on the south side of the pass. Here they selected the best feeding places possible and remained in corral until June before they could cross.

Meanwhile flour grew scarcer and prices, including those on all other foods as well, were soaring. Finally flour had mounted by daily advances of $5.00 until it brought $100 gold price or $200 in greenbacks. Hardtack sold for $1.35 a pound; bacon, $1.00; and salt, for fifty cents. Tobacco could scarcely be had at any price. Men were smoking a mixture of kinnikinnic and the white inside bark of cottonwood. Newsprint having run out, *The Montana Post* appeared on butcher paper.

At this point, when a bread riot seemed imminent, a committee of the citizens intervened in order to secure an equitable distribution of flour, prevent hoarding, and keep prices within reason. On Tuesday, April 18, 480 armed men appeared from Lower Town, marching in file and subject to orders of leaders on horseback. They were divided into companies, each under a captain, and carried empty flour-sacks for banners.

They searched all known sources of supply, agreeing to pay $27.00 per hundredweight for Salt Lake flour and $30.00 for "State." On Wednesday distribution of the flour at those prices took place. Each man willing to affirm he had no flour and could get none, received 12 pounds; double and triple rations were given to men with families. This was also done in Nevada and Junction, the whole proceedings being marked by very little disturbance.

Later it was found that some flour had been concealed and this was duly distributed. With wild meat plentiful at ten cents a pound and beef at twenty-five there was no longer any real suffering before supplies came in through the pass.

The coming of spring was attended by a pro-

longed rainy spell. The smaller streams became
raging torrents and the swamp between us and
East Gallatin was a veritable lake where muskrats
and beavers plied their tasks undisturbed.

We were all sleeping soundly one night when
Mrs. Ridgley was wakened suddenly by the drip-
ping of water on her side of the bed. She rose, lit
a candle, and proceeded to investigate. The drip-
ping became a trickle. She grabbed a milkpan
and put it on the bed to catch the water, calling to
the rest as she did so and cautioning Dad Ridgley
not to upset the pan. While we were slipping into
our things another leak claimed her attention. Soon
it became clear that there would not be enough
empty vessels to meet the need. We drew the beds
under the ridgepole, which seemed the driest place,
and covered everything we could with wagon canvas. Pools of water on different parts of the floor
grew larger until they met in one sixteen-by-twen-
ty puddle.

It was then that Mrs. Ridgley spoke her mind;
spoke it freely, pointedly. The last thing I heard
above the drip of water on the canvas over my
trundlebed was that no man in his senses had a
right to bring a woman into any such a place as
that.

Early next morning Dad Ridgley hied him to
a neighboring cow ranch where cowhides, which
were without market value, were to be had for the
asking; and from the fence next the stable he collected sufficient hides for his purpose. These he

piled into his light wagon, delivered at the house, and duly applied clapboard-wise to the roof, binding them with poles. It worked. After the surplus water stopped oozing from the ceiling, the floor began to dry, and harmony reigned once more.

When my store trousers wore out Mrs. Ridgley made me a brand new pair out of buckskin. Of these I was very proud. But alas for human vanity! During the first rainstorm I got them soaked. When they dried they grew hard and wrinkled. I soon began to feel "galded" in various strategic places, and was forced to shed them and work out the wrinkles before I could enjoy life once more.

We enclosed the forty that lay between us and the river with a rail fence of the "leaning" type. Not having to stop to dig post holes, we could put up quite a bit in a day. The sections were composed of posts at intervals of about eight feet, resting upon firm supports or "legs" and joined by three sixteen-foot poles fastened in place with wooden pins. Dad Ridgley broke up about ten acres in which we planted potatoes, cabbage, and rutabagas mostly, reserving a small piece for other vegetables. We got our plow made to order by a blacksmith in Virginia City. It was a twelve-inch. The share and mould-board were made of wagon irons and it cost $112.00. Dave Ballantyne got a fourteen-inch plow made for $140.00. We used a brush harrow.

In a belated extra edition of *The Montana Post* we read an article carrying the following head lines:

Virginia City, M. T., Saturday evening,
April 22, 1865. Telegraphic. The Best News Yet

Surrender of Lee and his whole force to General Grant. Jeff's whereabouts Uncertain!! Confederacy Gone Up!

General Anderson plants the same flag on Fort Sumter that he hauled down!

200 guns fired at each headquarters in honor of the victory.

At last the war was over. I wondered how many of our boys at home were among the missing. Opening my warsack that evening I drew out an envelope containing two folded sheets of paper whereon was copied in an exquisite hand the poem which I here give. The boyhood friend who gave it to me had answered the call to the colors. I have it yet, yellow with age.

The Two Soldiers

"It was just before the last fierce charge,
Two soldiers drew their rein;
With parting words and clasp of hands,
'We may never meet again.'

"One had blue eyes and curly hair,
Eighteen scarce a month ago,
And down his cheeks the tears did roll,
For he was only a boy, you know.

"The other was tall and dark and proud,
And his faith in this world was dim.
He only trusted the more in God,
For 'twas all the world to him.

"The tall, dark man was the first to speak,
Saying, 'Charley, my hour has come.
I wish you a little trouble would take,
For me when I am gone.

"I have a face upon my breast,
I shall wear it in the fight;
  With dark blue eyes and curly hair,
And she smiles like the morning light.

"Like the morning light was my love's
        fair face,
She gladdened my very life.
  And little did I care for the promise of
        fate,
When she promised to be my wife.'

"Tears filled the blue eyes of the boy,
He answered slow and dim,
  'I will do your bidding, comrade mine,
If I write back again.

"If you write back when I am gone
You must do as much for me.
  For mother at home must hear the news;
Pray tell her tenderly.'

"Just then the bugle sounded the charge,
In a moment hand clasped hand;
  Each answered, 'yes' as on they rushed,
Most brave, devoted band.

"They rode till they came to the crest of
        the hill,
When the rebels' shot and shell
  Poured a volley of death in their thinning
        ranks
And charged them as on they fell.

"Among the dead and the dying there
Lay the boy with the curly hair,

And the tall dark man that rode by his side
Lay dead beside him there.

"Now who will write to that blue-eyed girl
Those words that have been said,
    And who will write to that mother dear
That her only son is dead?"

Late snows in the nearby mountains forced the elk to seek new feeding grounds. During a big migration across the valley, I got my first one, a fat cow.

With the receipt of our paper, dated April 29, we read the words which threw a whole nation into sorrow. I give them as follows:

WASHINGTON, APRIL 14, AT 12 O'CLOCK.

This evening about 9 P. M. at Ford's Theatre, the president, while sitting in his private box with Mrs. Lincoln, Mrs. Harris, and Major Rathburne, was shot by an assassin who suddenly entered the box and approached behind the president. The assassin then leaped upon the stage, brandished a dagger, and made his escape in the rear of the theatre. A pistol ball entered the back of the president's head and penetrated nearly through the head. The wound is mortal. The president has been insensible ever since it was inflicted, and is now about dying.

At last we were to hear of the Sully expedition which was organizing at Sioux City when we came through. As soon as the roads were fit to travel a Mr. Dorr and his wife drove in from Sun river and took the claim just above Lon's. This couple had come through in the train which started under Sully's escort. When we told them how narrowly we missed going with Sully, they replied that we were very lucky we weren't along.

As well as I can recall it, I will briefly sketch the expedition, the purpose of which, as stated in a previous chapter, was to open a new route up the Missouri and Yellowstone rivers and across through Bozeman pass to the mines.

From Sioux City, on July 4, 1864, General Alfred Sully, with two army regiments and an emigrant train of 160 wagons, crossed the Missouri and proceeded up its western bank. Three days were consumed by the seven steamers in transporting them across.

Sully located Fort Rice on the west bank of the river. After eight days of work, eight hundred Missourian infantry were left to finish and garrison it.

From this point they struck west up Cannonball river to its head and across to Heart river. Here they engaged the Sioux under Dull Knife in a three-hour battle, in which the indians were routed.

Their progress southwestward up the Heart river to its source and through the Bad Lands of the Little Missouri was marked by skirmishes with the indians most of the way.

When they had arrived opposite old Fort Union, it was thought that the emigrants need not fear any more trouble with indians, and Sully with his command left them to go on by themselves. After fruitless engagements with the indians and wearied by long marches through drouth-ridden regions to the south, Sully and his command reached the Yellowstone. With much loss of equipment and horses they finally returned to the point of beginning late in the summer.

The emigrants pushed on up the Milk river to the Bear Paws. Arrived at Fort Benton, they continued along the old Mullan road to Sun river. Here the travel-worn emigrants finally located for the winter, September 21.

Mrs. Dorr told us that she would never forget their experience on Heart river. They were corraled, July 26, near Kildeer mountain. Sully, with his troops, had ridden southward a day or two earlier, presumably on the trail of redskins. Suddenly they were surrounded by a horde of hideously painted savages who charged with their customary blood-curdling warwhoops. But the watchful emigrants held them at bay until night when they contrived to send out messengers to Sully.

Throughout the night guards were alert for any effort on the part of the indians to steal upon the camp. In the morning they returned to the attack, but instead of attempting a sudden raid they kept up a desultory fire from a safe distance, thinking probably to harass or starve the whites into submission.

This lasted throughout the day. Suddenly, toward evening, the indians began retreating to their camp, where Sully and his forces, returning from the south, engaged them in battle and routed them completely. It was estimated that there were 1600 indians involved.

"They left everything and just kept on going," said Mrs. Dorr. "At their camp we found bolts of cloth and quantities of other plunder which they had got in raids along the Overland trail. There were also many scalps among their belongings. When we left, General Sully ordered the complete destruction of their camp."

Five or six miles up the river on the opposite side hunting parties of Bannacks and Snakes, returning from the Yellowstone, had made a large camp early in the spring. From their original stamping grounds on the upper courses of Snake river they followed our route as far as the Madison. Here they skirted the mountains and turned eastward through Bozeman pass, joining the Nez Percés on the Yellowstone. Why they had left so soon and pitched their tents down here in the settlement on the Nez Percés trail will be better understood after I have briefly reviewed some of the circumstances attending the Nez Percés' visit just previous to our coming. To Henry Davis, the lad who lived just across the swamp on East Branch, I am indebted for most of the details here given.

From their home in the Wallowa country old Chief Joseph led his band eastward for the great buffalo hunt. Shortly before our arrival they camped for a time in Gallatin valley. Their coming excited no alarm, for they had always been friendly toward the whites. It was their proud claim that they never had killed a white man.

Old Joseph was sitting in his tent one day, reading his Bible, when messengers came with news that two of his people, an old man and woman, had been wantonly murdered by white men. Joseph immediately called his people in council. It taxed his splendid powers of leadership to restrain them from hasty action. But there was no resisting their demand for justice. Wishing to follow a course that would be fair to indians and whites alike, he dispatched messengers at once to John J. Thomas, a justice of the peace, informing him of the deed and asking that the murderers be taken and punished. Judge Thomas, wholly in sympathy with the indians, told them to follow the men themselves, and not to lose any time about it.

"And if we catch them?" they asked.

"Do anything you like with them," was his answer.

A band of Nez Percés at once set out in pursuit. They trailed the murderers as far as Virginia City where they disappeared and the indians had to return without them.

The Nez Percés then moved over to the Yellowstone. Here they were joined by the Snakes and Bannacks. All went well for a time until a band of River Crows appeared on the scene, when trouble arose over some ponies. During the fracas that followed the Crows, Snakes, and Bannacks, thoroughly spanked, pulled stakes for other parts.

The Crows headed for the Musselshell, and the Snakes and Bannacks for the Gallatin. It is probable that while here they sued for peace, for runners between their camp and the Yellowstone were frequent.

One afternoon in early May before high water, as I was returning from the field, I saw the advance riders of what looked like a vast army approaching from the east. In a moment I knew it was the returning Nez Percés, for their coming had been heralded days before. Fearing trouble might arise over the last summer's affair, Old Joseph had sent a band of radicals back to Washington by a roundabout way just before the main party started.

My first concern was that our horses which were grazing out in the open might get mixed up with the indian ponies and follow them off. In a few minutes I had started them in toward the corral, when half a dozen indians galloped up, singing as they rode.

"Me help?" their spokesman asked.

"Yes, please," I answered; and in a jiffy they had corraled the horses and were back for a minute's chat before they joined their companions. One of them wore an enormous head piece of buffalo horns and eagle feathers. All of them were more or less be-feathered and brilliant in peace-time paint. They wore buckskin, oramented with beads and quill work, bits of scarlet cloth showed in their braids, and they carried light weapons of the chase.

The indians advanced in large family groups or

clans, each with its separate equipment and ponies. Over the plain for miles, it seemed to me, I could see their deep, irregular file. In each party were pack animals laden with buckskin sacks of dried buffalo meat. If one of them chanced to stray, it was promptly hustled back in place. Ponies harnessed to travois plodded along with their varied burdens; these might be house-hold goods, puppies, papooses, the aged, or the infirm. Two or three tepee-poles were usually strapped to each side of the saddle; the saddle being held in place by a girth and breastband. The carrier of buckskin or other hide was bound between the poles. Sometimes a pack was strapped on the saddle; occasionally a squaw or papoose rode the horse. They served their purpose well. I have ridden in wheeled vehicles that had nothing on them for safety and comfort.

On they marched with Old Chief Joseph at their head, a pageant of barbaric splendor, this caravan of the wilderness. We watched them for an hour or more until they disappeared around a bend in the river toward the ford.

Later in the evening we could hear the rythmic beat of tom-toms coming faintly from their village beside the camp of Bannacks and Snakes.

Next morning it was noised around the neighborhood that all who wished to attend would be welcome at the ceremonial of the burying of the hatchet to be held that day. There would be a big pow-wow – speeches and a feast, followed by a

THE TRAVOIS TRAIL

Reproduced from an original drawing made by Captain Seth Eastman about 1851

dance. The Nez Percés were to be the hosts and would furnish the eats.

Nearly everyone in the valley went that afternoon. Now when indians are "at home" to their friends, it's very likely to be a leisurely affair. No one ever hurries. And this was to be no exception to the rule. All available kettles were filled with dried buffalo meat and jerked venison and set cooking hours in advance. There was much skirmishing about for firewood and disciplining of small children and dogs who showed undue interest in the proceedings. The very young and the very old, too hungry to wait, were munching pieces of the raw dried meat. Choke-cherries, crushed seeds and all and dried, were boiled, then strained so that the "soup" would be free from broken pits.

Meanwhile boys on little pinto ponies were scurrying after straying horses or running races in the open. The rank and file of the men were gathering in the area bounded by the two camps, where they sat in semi-circular rows facing a shelter erected for the old men, chieftains, and medicine men. Women and children chose a position at one side nearest the fires.

There was an announcement by the "master of ceremonies" attended by a brief beat of tom-toms. Followed speeches at considerable length, each marked at important points by loud grunts of approbation and all interspersed with drum-beats.

Nothing was intelligible to the white visitors, except the spirit of good will prevailing.

Then the hatchet – in this case of stone and made for the occasion – was produced with great circumstance and buried very deep. Not a sound interrupted this rite. When the last bit of earth was pressed over the spot, the bond was sealed, and a thrill of excitement ran over the crowd. The peace pipe now went the rounds.

The speeches and protestations of friendship which followed were terminated by the appearance of the kettles of meat. Every one received a generous portion, with more to follow when that was eaten. All ceremony was laid aside as the feast progressed, and at its conclusion one felt that "a very pleasant time was had."

At sunset the dance began. There is nothing so weirdly beautiful as the old tribal dances; the flash of weapons, the tinkle of bells, the riot of barbaric color, the savage grace of the dancers in perfect measure with the rythmic beat of the tom-toms and their own songs of prowess. I have always been deeply impressed with the forms of the indian dance; but as for their significance, though "every little movement has a meaning all its own," the meaning, alas, is sealed to me.

All night long, by the mellow fire light, the dance continued and the great circle of dusky onlookers remained unbroken. In the intervals the old announcer would proclaim that some one would give gifts or that a new dance was about to begin. His voice never seemed to tire.

Old Joseph stood for peace, both with his kind

SURRENDER OF CHIEF JOSEPH
From an original painting by E. A. Paxson in the
state capitol, Montana

and with the pale-face. His qualities of leadership were only equalled by his capacity for friendship. All who knew him loved him. Every inch an indian, he was every inch a man. And the young lad, his son, whom we know as the late Chief Joseph, nobly followed in his father's footsteps. Charged with the task of keeping the homeland safe for his people, he responded in a manner which gives him a place unique as a leader of men. Though his cause was lost, who can say that he failed?

Chapter XV
Concerning Various Things

Concerning Various Things

The settlers on East Branch had raised their crop by irrigation in 1864. It is likely that the idea was borrowed from the Mormons at Salt Lake, where irrigation was introduced at the outset. A meeting was called in our neighborhood late in the spring and an organization effected for the purpose of constructing and maintaining a ditch from the McCormick brothers' place, nearly five miles above the crossing, to our place. There were fourteen members in all, as follows, Paul and John Mc-Cormick, the two Wells brothers, the two Falls brothers, Doc Robinson, Charley Blakely, Kirkendahl, Eisentroutt, Dorr, Deacon Smith, Alonzo, and Ridgley.

At the intake a six or seven-foot cut was necessary and for nearly half a mile it was pretty hard digging, mostly pick and shovel work. Then we used the plows and a home-made scraper or "stone-boat," a v-shaped affair of timbers, constructed the width of the ditch and weighted. Several furrows were plowed and the stone-boat, drawn by six or eight horses, followed and threw the dirt out at each side.

Mrs. Ridgley didn't see why we needed to irrigate. She didn't believe it would ever quit raining.

But by the time the ditch was finished and the water in it, our crops were ready to be watered.

On his return trip from Virginia City with the plow and a bill of groceries, Dad Ridgley visited the Slade place near the Madison. The house was of stone, with thick walls like a fortress, pierced with loopholes. Here Slade and his band must have felt secure after one of their tempestuous visits to town.

Although the Slade affair was fresh in the minds of the people when we passed through Virginia City, I have purposely reserved mention of it for a later place rather than in the account of the road agents. Slade belongs in a class by himself. So much has been said and written of him that it is difficult to determine where fact leaves off and fiction begins. Therefore I shall simply review what was common knowledge to us at that time.

We first heard of Slade as a train-master on the Overland route to California. The fear that he had aroused through his reckless daring and desperate deeds of bloodshed was only equalled by the admiration he inspired by his generous acts and his great efficiency as an overland officer. He was the most feared and the most loved man on the line.

At that time a Frenchman by the name of Jules was station keeper at Julesberg, on the South Platte, just over the Colorado line. Jules bore an unsavory reputation, and to save itself from the heavy losses sustained through his mismanagement and dishonesty, the company appointed Slade division agent. This was a lucky choice for the company, but the beginning of a deadly feud between Jules and Slade.

A quarrel over a team soon arose. Slade recovered the team which he alleged Jules had appropriated, but carried away some buckshot from Jules's gun. Healed of his wound, Slade sought out Jules at a ranch where it was reported the latter was hidden. Tying him up to a post, he spent most of the day shooting up his helpless enemy, fortifying himself meanwhile from his hip flask. As proof of his prowess he carried the dead man's ears in his vest pocket for years afterwards.

As an example of his Robin Hood generosity, we were told on Sweetwater, Slade visited summary justice upon a couple of murderers and wife abductors and took the murdered man's wife and child under his protection. Smith and Bacon, who ran a ranch and store fifteen miles below Independence Rock, were the culprits. Having murdered a man by the name of Bartholomew, they carried the wife and child to their ranch. Mrs. Bartholomew with her child made her way to Plante's store and station at the crossing of the Sweetwater near Independence Rock, called in those days the crossing of the Lone Rock river. Here Slade found them and took them at once to his wife. Then, seeking out the murderers, he hanged them, sold their ranch and other interests and turned the money over to the widow. Mrs. Slade meanwhile fitted them out with clothes suitable for travel, Slade gave them passes over his line, and soon they were on their way to relatives in the East.

A blacksmith by the name of Robinson, from one of the stations, told us years afterwards that he had incurred Slade's ill will after the Jules affair. Slade sent word to Robinson that he intended to "get" the latter the first chance he had; whereupon Robinson, having once got a sight of Jules's ears in Slade's possession, and not wishing to add his own to the collection, took the next coach for Bannack.

Such was the man who moved over in 1863 and built his stronghold on the Madison where he and his pals lorded it over the inhabitants of Virginia City and the other camps whenever they got thirsty and rode in for "refreshments."

Though no robber himself, nor ever charged with murder in the territory, his past deeds and the terror he inspired when "on the rampage" determined the citizens to check his mad career in the interest of social order and personal safety.

The Vigilantes had cleared the camps of road agents and having assisted in restoring the miners' court, disbanded. Slade rode into Virginia City one evening, got drunk and started shooting the town up – "raising hell generally," the citizens told us. An officer arrested him next day. He tore up the warrant and stamped upon it, his armed companions standing by to support him.

This was the excuse the Vigilantes needed. Hastily reorganizing, they sent a messenger to him advising him to leave town at once or they would take him in hand.

He sought out Judge Davis and with drawn derringer, threatened his life if they touched him.

Following a meeting of the Virginia City branch, the Vigilantes of Nevada accompanied by almost all of the miners, joined them and assumed the initiative. Slade's actions had been tolerated too long; nothing but his immediate execution would satisfy them. Accordingly, he was arrested without delay and informed of his doom. He weakened at once and pleaded for clemency. The committee remained firm. A beam was laid across the gate posts of a corral just above the intersection of the two creeks. A drygoods box served for a platform. Knowing his popularity and that every minute lost added to his chances for rescue, they took him at once to this improvised scaffold.

Meanwhile a messenger sped to the ranch to inform Mrs. Slade of his arrest. The best horsewoman in the country and owning the fleetest horse, she sprang into the saddle and began her race with death. She had saved him once before and she could do so again – if only she reached him in time! She was a woman of rare grace and charm, of great courage and sympathy.

Her personal influence was fully appreciated by both factions. One party played desperately for time; the other strove as desperately to expedite matters. Law and order and personal right were again at stake. There were entreaties, last-minute-requests, frantic attempts at delay. The beginnings of a demonstration were instantly checked by the guard with levelled guns, while the condemned man gave final directions concerning business matters.

The fatal noose was then adjusted, the command given, – "Men, do your duty," and Slade swung at the end of the rope, a corpse.

They carried him inside and were laying him out when Mrs. Slade rode up. Learning that all was over she gave way completely for a moment. As she dismounted someone asked her what she intended to do with the gun she was carrying.

"I was going to shoot him if necessary to keep him from being hanged," was the answer. And in another moment she was with the remains of her idol.

Finishing our part of the ditch, tending the crops, looking after the stock and the numerous other tasks about the farm, filled our time, so that fall was upon us before we realized it. Mrs. Ridgley's butter money was our only cash income during the summer before the vegetables were ready for market. We were milking three cows. Butter brought $2.00 in gold-dust at first; later it got down to ninety cents.

During the fore part of October an expedition under command of Colonel James A. Sawyer visited Bozeman en route to Virginia City, arriving there October 14. So far as I can learn very little is known of the Sawyer expedition of that year.

Thinking it worthy of more than passing mention, I shall summarize the main features of the enterprise. I am indebted to Albert M. Holman, of Sergeant Bluff, Iowa, for most of the facts here given. Mr. Holman was a teamster in the expedition. Fifty years later he visited us at my home in the Big Horns, beside the Bozeman trail, and we spent a pleasant week talking over old times and visiting portions of the route.

The expedition consisted of the Sawyer train and a military escort. In this train were fifteen wagons, each with three yoke of oxen; eighteen trail or double wagons, drawn by six yoke of oxen; the drivers, guides, engineer, a man who acted as surgeon, geologist and botanist, wagon masters, Colonel Sawyer and his secretary, besides a few emigrants. The government provided them with an escort consisting of parts of two companies of infantry made up of "Galvanized Yankees," or paroled rebel soldiers, and a detachment of twenty-five Dakota cavalrymen. They brought a six-inch howitzer along.

The government financed the project, allowing about $80,000 for opening a wagon route from Sioux City to Virginia City. This was to be known as the Niobrara-Virginia City wagon road, and would effect a saving of about five-hundred miles between the two points, it was thought.

The latter part of May, Colonel Sawyer and his party crossed the Missouri with cattle and wagons, proceeded to Niobrara, farther up the river near the mouth of the Niobrara river, or Running Water, where they loaded up, secured their escort, and organized for the expedition.

Leaving Niobrara, they followed the Running Water through the Sand hills for about three hundred twenty-five miles, bore northwest across White river and Hat creek, and halted upon a tributary of the Cheyenne near the southern extremity of the Black hills. Here they remained for ten days while a detachment of twenty soldiers rode down to Fort Laramie to get shoes for the nearly barefoot soldiers.

When the ten days were up and the soldiers hadn't put in an appearance, the expedition pulled on, expecting them to catch up later. This they did several days later when all hopes of seeing them again were given up. At sight of the camp fires late in the evening they heralded their return with a volley of shots and hilarious yelling. The men at the camp, mistaking them for indians, fired in the general direction of the noise. The mistake was likely to prove serious until someone rode in ahead and announced their approach in simpler terms.

They followed the Cheyenne nearly to its source, then struck out westward across the rough country toward Powder river, suffering greatly for want of water in the Powder river mountains. After three days of this, they found a stagnant pool. When the oxen were turned loose they rushed into the water, stirring it up so that they could scarcely drink it.

Next day a detachment of one-third of the men were chosen by lot to drive the loose stock to Powder river. While watering there they discovered lurking indians, and about midnight they returned with the stock. It was now decided to return to the Cheyenne and take a new start.

A few miles south of the present Gillette, Wyoming, Nat Hedges, a young emigrant of the party, who was taking a $20,000 stock of merchandise out to the mines, was shot from his horse by indians while looking for water.

They pushed southward into the Pumpkin Butte country where they came upon fresh wagon tracks following a dry fork of Powder river. They knew that General Connor had been sent north from Laramie that spring and thought he might have gone this way. The appearance of indians now caused them to turn back again.

Returning to within ten miles of the North Fork of the Cheyenne (Belle Fourche) they were attacked and forced to corral for defense. After a three-days' siege the indians suddenly ran up a white flag. A truce was concluded, the indians promising to leave peaceably, provided the whites would give them some provisions. This was done and they left. A roll was called and two men were found missing. One was discovered near the flag of truce, scalped; the other was never found.

The reason for the indians' sudden desire for peace was soon learned. General Connor was just then on his way back from the Yellowstone in what was known as the Powder river expedition. Hearing the shots, he had sent a detachment in our direction. It was the approach of these soldiers that had decided the indians to make terms advantageous to themselves while the Sawyer party were yet unaware of Connor's nearness.

When Connor's men came up, they accompanied the Sawyer party to the newly-built Fort Connor (later re-named Fort Reno), some twelve miles distant on Powder river. Here they stayed a week to rest up. Before they left they exchanged their escort for part of two companies of Michigan cavalry.

In the meantime Connor had met a band of indians, mostly Arapahoes under Black Bear and Old David, and had routed them on Tongue river, near the present Ranchester. At this time Bridger was attached to the command.

The Sawyer party now moved northwestward from Fort Connor, across Clear Creek and on to the present site of Sheridan, where they joined the Bozeman trail. From here they proceeded to Wolf creek. Before they reached Tongue river, Captain Cole was shot by indians while riding ahead on Wolf creek divide. On Tongue river, midway between Ranchester and Dayton, they lay in corral fourteen days, besieged by the enemy. Two more men were killed. The three bodies were wrapped

in blankets and placed in one grave, while some of
the men played fiddles and danced jigs in one of
the tents to divert the attention of a number of indians who had come in under a truce for a parley.
Cattle were then driven over the grave to hide the
traces.

A relief party from Fort Connor, summoned by
messengers sent under cover of the darkness, appeared in due time and routed the indians, des-
troying their camp. Sawyer now followed the
Bozeman route to Virginia City where the men
were paid off and the expedition disbanded. They
had been nearly five months on the journey, were
besieged twenty-five days in all, lost six men, and
covered 1039 miles by odometer measure.

Sawyer led an expedition over the same route
the following year, of which accounts are extant.
This road was never used to any extent; increasing
troubles with the indians and the building of the
Union Pacific railroad were probably main causes
for the abandonment of this and other roads across
the territory then known as the Powder river region.

As soon as the rutabagas and the early cabbage
and potatoes were ready to gather, we loaded two
wagons and, in company with Smith's and another
neighbor having produce to sell, set out for Helena,
ninety miles away. We crossed at the new ford
just below our place, followed the main Gallatin
past old Gallatin City on the opposite side, ferried
across the Missouri just below the junction of the

Madison and Jefferson, and struck west across the tableland toward Helena.

The first night we came to a warm spring creek where the oxen refused to drink, and we drove about nine miles farther, where we found good water and made a late camp. We thought that some day those warm springs might be converted into baths.

We arrived at Helena early the fifth day and camped down below the town on Prickly Pear creek. After dinner we all went up town. We sold most of our stuff for cash to Simpson and Vivian, who kept a large general store well up in town. Boone Simpson and Jim Vivian were brothers respectively of our neighbors, John Simpson and Bob Vivian, and were among the freighters who were marooned the winter before beyond the pass.

As I strolled along the street I passed a little ten-by-twelve shack literally packed with Chinamen; there were four lying asleep on the floor and two asleep in a bunk above them. Nearing a butcher shop I saw several customers hurrying home with pieces of meat impaled on sticks. There was evidently a shortage of wrapping paper. Claims were staked out all over the townsite, apparently. The water was all diverted from the creek bed and every foot of ground except in the streets and where the buildings stood was being sluiced. I noticed one claim particularly where they had dug to a depth of twelve or fifteen feet. A platform was suspended midway of the pit, by which men with shovels relayed the dirt from the bottom to the sluice above.

Last Chance Gulch, where Helena is located, was discovered by John Cowan and his party from Colorado, July 21, 1864. Having prospected in vain for some time they were about to give up when someone suggested that they take a last chance over here; hence the name. When we saw it first, Helena was a well-built, flourishing place second only to Virginia City in size. About $16,000,000 in gold was taken out the first year.

Shortly following our return from Helena, reports came from there of another execution, that of James Daniels, for the murder of a man by the name of Gartley, during a quarrel over a game of cards. The Vigilantes arrested him and turned him over to the civil authorities. He was given a prison sentence for manslaughter, but was illegally reprieved after a short time by the acting governor on petition of some of the citizens. Returning to Helena, he began making threats against the witnesses who testified against him. Judge Munson then ordered his re-arrest; but to facilitate matters the Vigilantes took him in hand and hanged him that night. Mrs. Gartley died from the shock of her husband's murder.

In this connection it is interesting to note the dependence which was placed in the Vigilantes even after courts were well established. In the Histori-

cal Society of Montana *Contributions* we read that
a Grand Jury of one of the districts presented to
the Court in lieu of an indictment:

That it is better to leave the punishment of the criminal
offenders to the Vigilantes, who always act impartially, and
who would not permit the escape of proved criminals on tech-
nical and absurd grounds.

The rush to Helena and fresh discoveries in
Confederate Gulch were signals for the lawless
element to begin operations anew. The first notable case was that of two ruffians, Harry Slater and
John Keene. They quarreled first in Salt Lake
City, and meeting in Helena previous to our visit,
renewed their quarrel which terminated in Keene's
shooting Slater in cold blood. Yielding to the popular demand for a citizens' trial, the sheriff turned
Keene over to the Vigilantes. The trial was brief,
followed by his execution in Dry Gulch at midnight, "X" Beidler officiating.

The Helena branch of the committee now reor-
ganized regularly. They were soon busy with the
case of Jake Silvie of Diamond City. Silvie, alias
Jacob Seachrist, was implicated with Jem Kelly
in a murder on Snake river when we came through.
It was said that he had murdered twelve men in
as many years. Being arrested for a series of robberies in Diamond City, he confessed various other
crimes and was promptly taken to Helena, convicted and escorted to the historic tree in Dry Gulch.

Road agents were again active beyond Virginia
City. About the middle of July the stage coach

bound for Salt Lake was held up in Portneuf canyon. Four men were killed, two were injured, and one escaped unhurt. The driver, who proved to be a road agent himself, also escaped uninjured. The robber got away with $65,000 in gold. We heard that the driver was caught and executed by the Denver branch, and that the Vigilantes were hot on the trail of the others in the Kootenai region. This affair stirred up the whole country. Except for a few rare cases, however, the wave of crime was at an end. "X" Beidler's famous trip to Salt Lake and points in the southwest in quest of a criminal, whom he brought back single-handed, helped to increase respect for the law.

At the November election, the following men were elected to office: Clerk, William M. Wright; Sheriff, J. S. Mendenhall; Treasurer, P. W. McAdow; Probate Judge, J. M. Bozeman; Assessor, George D. Thomas; Surveyor, F. K. Meredith; District-attorney, J. H. Shober; Commissioners, Philip Thorpe, A. F. Nichols, and D. H. Ketcham. The first legislature met at Bannack, December 12, 1864. Gallatin county was created February 2, 1865, with East Gallatin as the county seat. During this session also the public school system was organized and a civil and criminal code of practice established. The supreme court, which was organized four days before the first territorial election, consisted of three members, a chief justice and two associate justices, who acted also as district judges in the three districts created at that

time. There were also an attorney, a marshal, and
two deputies, one of whom was J. X. – or "X" –
Beidler, who achieved such prominence in bringing criminals to justice.

Along about threshing time a band of Crows
camped on East Branch just above Bozeman. They
used to come over our way sometimes and beg.
Farmers were busy cradling their grain, tying it
in bundles by hand, and hauling it into the stack
yard. Frequently two or more would stack their
grain together where fields were too small to make
a new "set"at every farm. One horsepower threshing machine served the whole community. It
was above Bozeman one day, a day long remembered in the valley. Saddle horses belonging to the
threshing crew were grazing nearby. Of a sudden
mounted indians dashed in between the horses and
the machine, headed the bunch toward the river,
and were out of range quicker than it takes to tell
it. Shots were exchanged before they disappeared
in the timber, but without effect on either side.

Nearly every herd of loose saddle stock was
raided that day. We got our first inkling that anything was wrong late that afternoon. I had come
up from the garden where we were working, to get
a bucket of fresh water at the spring. Three young
indians came along and wanted some "grease" for
their revolvers. I got them some oil and they walked on up toward the Dorr place.

Mrs. Dorr was alone, her husband having joined
the threshing crew. The indians went in without

knocking and asked for some matches. Mrs. Dorr gave them some, expecting them to leave, but they seemed in no hurry to go. Something in their behavior now filled her with a vague alarm. Observing her nervousness they exchanged amused glances and one of them approached her. She quickly slipped past him, went outside, and cupping her fingers, called to her husband in the direction of the barn. This simple ruse had the desired effect, for they left immediately. Mrs. Dorr spent the rest of the day with us until her husband's return.

It was estimated that about fifty head of horses altogether were driven out of the country. How ours escaped I don't know. All was now excitement. A raid on the horses might mean a raid on the inhabitants later. A visit was paid to the indian camp. The indians were very much surprised over the affair, showed deep concern, and were most eager to assist. It was Flatheads, without a doubt, they said; Flatheads had been prowling around of late. And to prove their good faith they sent riders out to scour the country in search of the thieves and stolen horses.

A meeting of the settlers was hastily called which resulted in a decision to build a defense where the people might take refuge in case of an attack. Accordingly work was begun at once on a stockade on East Gallatin just across the swamp from our place. Practically the whole neighborhood turned out to push things along.

Two or three days later Charley Smith came

back from Virginia City with the mail. He was batching up on West Gallatin at the time. At once he missed his favorite white saddle-horse which he had turned out with a bunch that ranged down toward Dorr's. Of no particular breed, he was a fine, spirited animal that responded with every ounce of his strength to kindly treatment. Faithful companion of years, Charley had been favoring him of late and was using a younger horse, a bay, on the trips to Virginia City.

Certain that the horse was stolen, Charley got busy. He tried to find volunteers to go with him in search of the horses, but every available man seemed to be working on the stockade. He rode over there. They told him of their visit to the Crow camp where it was alleged that a renegade band of Flatheads had done the mischief.

"Oh bosh! It's no Flatheads. It's nothing but the Crows," he replied. "I've had experience with Crows before."

They explained that some of the indians were out on their trail. But no one could make him believe it was Flatheads, and he rode home.

The Crows soon reported the return of the party with one of the guilty Flatheads, whom they were holding under close guard. A council would be held immediately to decide his fate. It was shortly announced that the culprit would be burned at the stake the following day. The public was invited. Preparations for the event were going forward with much bustle and noise. Chance visitors must have been duly impressed with the sorry doom that awaited the guilty one. With great ceremony the stake was driven and the fire-wood piled around it, ready to be lighted. But when the next day dawned, the bird had flown. Fate was cheated.

The whole thing was so transparent that feeling ran high. The indians were asked to "pike" and they "piked." Work on the stockade was speeded up.

Unable to persuade anyone to go along, Charley Smith decided to ride down to the Musselshell alone after his horse. Before he started he came over to our place and got a supply of powder and buckshot. When he left no one expected to see him back alive. The story of what happened, as it reached us by piece-meal, was as follows:

Riding into the Crow village on the Musselshell, Charley asked for the chief. He came, and Charley demanded his horse. The Crows had taken it; he knew it was there, and he had come to get it.

At first the chief disclaimed any knowledge of the horse. But Charley was in no mood to temporize; he hadn't ridden two hundred fifty miles for nothing. Tapping his scabbard, he told the indian that if the horse was not produced at once, he would signal his waiting companions and they would charge the camp. The chief then signed for the horse to be brought, and Charley led him out of the camp in triumph a few minutes later.

Within an hour's ride of Diamond City, on the return trip, they crossed a small creek traversing a marshy place. As they picked their way to firmer ground, the horse Charley was riding stumbled and fell, throwing him forward. The gun discharged and sent the full load of buckshot tearing through his shoulder. He lurched to the ground.

By the merest chance two hunters, riding in this lonely region, heard the shot and hastened up. There they found him crumpled in a heap. The horses were standing nearby. They believed his life was ebbing away and they asked him if he had any message to leave.

"Just take me to the creek and wash my shoulder and tie it up," was the answer. "I'm not going to die."

They tore up shirts, cleansed the wound, and bound it as best they could; then, improvising a litter of blankets secured between two saddle-horses, they started for Diamond City. It was said that after a little he was able to sit in the saddle with the support of a man at each side, when they could proceed faster.

Arrived at Diamond City, he received the best of care, and in an incredibly short time, due in great part to his strong will and splendid vitality, he was healed of his wound and ready to come home.

I was out in the yard one forenoon. The folks were away that day. Someone was coming up the river. It was Charley, riding the bay and leading his white horse, just as though nothing had happened. That goes to show that you couldn't keep a good man down – when that man was Charley Smith.

Chapter XVI
On the Bosom of the Great Muddy

On the Bosom of the Great Muddy

We were moving again, or more strictly speaking, yet. For it was written in the stars that our advent into the valley was to be but the beginning of a series of moves, ending with the purchase of the farm at the upper crossing, ten miles above, on the Bozeman-Virginia City road. If we had kept chickens, I am sure they would have crossed their legs in anticipation as is said to be the habit of chickens that have weathered a succession of moves. A road-house and toll bridge went with the farm. Mrs. Ridgley's cooking traditions and the good prices received for our produce were responsible for the choice of this location on the main highway.

The first link in the chain of events was the sale of our place to Boone Simpson, of Helena. Due to failing health he was giving up business for farm life.

Before giving possession we loaded up two wagons with what produce we had to spare, and in company with Deacon Smith, started for Diamond City. We drove one yoke of oxen to each wagon. All went well until we took the fifteen-mile ridge road after leaving the valley road below Gallatin City. At the steepest place we put the three yoke on the forward wagon and had proceeded only a little way when they all stopped of their own accord. They yielded neither to persuasion, force, nor guile, but stood stock-still in their tracks. We blocked the wheels and gave ourselves over to pleasant reflections.

When even the deacon seemed about to use strong language and history repeat itself, a horseman rode up and offered his services, adding that he had had some experience with oxen.

"All right," replied Dad Ridgley; "they've simply quit on us. Mebbe it's the strange road and the steep climb. We've drove em a long ways and they've never acted that way before."

The newcomer got off his horse, picked up a short stick, prodded each ox lightly, talking to them gently all the while; then stepping back, he gave a sharp command to go forward, and they all moved as one. He drove them over the steep place while we stood and watched them performing perfectly for a stranger. And we thought we knew how to handle oxen!

We drove the other wagons up without any more trouble and were soon on our way again. From this ridge one got a magnificent view of the three forks of the Missouri and the valley beyond. We approached Diamond City by a road cut into the canyon side through frequent beds of shale and slate. Most of the houses were roofed with slate. The camp was smaller than the other mining towns we had visited and stretched irregularly up and down the gulch. The country was rough and there were few roads. Everything had to be packed out to the farther diggings. I noted one string of burros loaded with beef, each carrying a quarter on either side and only their heads and tails visible.

The first night out on the return trip, we decided to camp just below Gallatin City where the road ran nearest the river. Delayed by a loosening tire, I had fallen half a mile behind the others when suddenly the air was alight with meteors. They fell all about me, bursting into a myriad of fire-fragments and filling the air with detonations. Whizzing past my face, crashing at my feet, blinding me, they were a pursuing fate and I their helpless victim, alone with my terrified oxen. Every moment I felt would be my last, should a meteorite strike me; and yet I was caught by the beauty and wonder of it when great balls of fire, bursting, sprinkled the sky with star-dust which glowed for a moment, then slowly faded into the night. A half hour, I judged, it lasted, then ceased as abruptly as it had begun.

November 13 – the night the stars fell! My elders could proudly date back to the November 12, 1833, when the stars fell in the East. An old darky in North La Crosse had even kept a friend out of jail when charged with voting under age at the election following the Emancipation Proclamation.

"Ah know he's ob age," he testified, "case he was bawn de night de stahs fell."

I, too, could count time from the night the stars fell.

Shortly before we gave possession and moved in with the boys on the next ranch below for the winter, they decided to have a "gethering" at their place. It was the first real party on the West Gallatin and all seemed bent on making the most of it. The guests began arriving early and the ladies left mysterious boxes and pans covered with tea-towels in Georgeanna's keeping before being ushered into the big room where Uncle Harrison was tinkering with his fiddle.

After he had adjusted a new string and with much thrumming and scraping got the instrument tuned to his satisfaction, he struck into a lively air, to which some of the boys responded by making the rafters rattle in a real old time hoe-down.

Quadrilles were coming in strong just then, although the scarcity of ladies was a considerable handicap. However, there was usually a boy in the offing who was willing to submit to the white handkerchief round his arm, which would change his sex temporarily and insure the completion of the set. Sometimes complications arose, as for instance when this same youth, forgetting that he was a girl for the time being, would "alaman" in the wrong direction, there to stand helplessly watching the couple before him balance and swing while his partner teetered forlornly on another "corner" of the circle. If worst came to worst Uncle Harrison would stop a moment while the caller jumped in, unscrambled the dancers, and readjusted them so that the dance could go on.

There were several who could do the Rye waltz, schottische, and polka, and there was a couple or two who could even essay the Spanish varsovienne, called in these parts the "vasoovianna."

"Refreshments" were served at midnight. If my memory hasn't played me tricks, they consisted of fried chicken from the cattle ranch, salad and pickles provided by Mrs. Blakely, one of Mrs. Ridgley's cream layer-cakes, plates of Georgeanna's beaten biscuits, "jell," coffee. Conversation waxed as our hunger decreased. Vard, Dave, and Bob sat in a corner with the two young ladies from the ranch where we got the hides for our roof. Dave and Vard presently got into an argument over a point of grammar. Unable to settle it themselves, they gallantly decided to leave it to the younger of the girls.

"Are you a grammarian?" asked Vard.

"No, sir," she replied demurely, "I'm a Missourian."

After the plates were taken up games were introduced. Forfeits came first with charades a close second. "Picking grapes" was the unanimous choice of the boys to begin with. If you've never picked grapes, my dear reader, you don't know what you've missed. In this game whoever is "it" stands upon a chair while those of the opposite sex gather in a line at each side. A kiss is then bestowed on each alternately to left and to right, and the "grapes" are "picked." If any one weakens, a forfeit is due. I think we ended our games with tintin.

Then, before dancing was resumed, there were songs, most of them sad and very long. My own voice was changing and I had range enough to attempt even the most difficult of our national airs – if I could have carried a tune in a gunny-sack. As it was, my only vocal effort was Yankee Doodle; people were willing to forgive me my queer tones provided I could:

> Mind the music and the step
> And with the girls be handy.

Mr. Ridgley's favorite, which was also very long, and pointed out a moral, but was not specially sad, began,

> Come all ye folks that have peanuts
> And give your neighbors none,
>   Oh you can't have any of my peanuts
> When your peanuts are gone,—
>   When your peanuts are gone,
>   When your peanuts are gone,
> Oh you can't have any of my peanuts
>   When your peanuts are gone.

A folk-song which we used to act out at the "play parties" back in Wisconsin, created a great deal of amusement. Part of it runs as follows:

> Oh don't you remember the night
> We sat under the juniper tree,
>   Heigh-o!

> The old man came out with his old rusty gun
> And swore he would shoot us if we didn't run,
>   Heigh-o,   heigh-o!
> And didn't we run,
>   Heigh-o!

It was nearly daylight when the party broke up and we took leave of the boys and Georgeanna and Uncle Harrison, who had given us such a happy time. I wonder if there are any alive besides myself who were there that night.

Two items in our paper interested us, each in its own way. One was a clipping from the Salt Lake Enterprise and ran as follows:

> Died, Bishop Ephraim Kinall Blair (appropriate eulogies) leaving nine wives, and forty-three small children. In the midst of wives we sometimes kick the bucket.

The other item had to do with the indian question in our region. It bore the date of December 6, 1865, and runs in part:

> Treaty with the Blackfeet, Fort Benton, November 17, 1865 . . . and so was concluded a treaty in the highest degree satisfactory to the whites which gives over to us all the vast extent of country embracing between 200,000 and 300,000 square miles, in which are situated our largest towns, Helena, Virginia City, Bannack, each, and containing all our rich mines.

(The northern part of the Indian territory was designated as their dwelling place and the southern part to the Musselshell as their hunting grounds, as included in the treaty with the Blackfeet, of

October 17, 1855. The Gros Ventres, Piegans, and Bloods were represented with the Blackfeet.)

This was great news and marked an important step forward in our relations with the tribes to the west and north of us.

The winter passed quickly and pleasantly with us. I spent most of my spare time with my traps. We lived in one room of the house, the boys in the other. The rooms were large and there was a loft overhead which the boys reserved for themselves. Our plans were to sell the cattle, store the household goods, and return to Wisconsin in the spring; then, after arranging their affairs so that they could leave permanently, the Ridgleys would bring back another load or two of household goods and take possession of the place at the upper crossing. I fully intended to come back with them.

On a morning late in May, 1866, we started for Fort Benton with the ponies, light wagon, and only our camp equipment. A man and his family who had wintered in the valley, joined us on their way to Iowa. We intended crossing at the nearest ford, but changed our minds when we got there. Two wagons, heavily loaded and drawn by several yoke of oxen, had preceded us a little way. The wagon ahead barely made it across. The second wagon was midway of the stream when all but the tongue-yoke broke loose. We got there in time to see it roll over, freeing the struggling wheelers, and stranding on a snag farther down. They managed to rope it and drag it ashore before we left.

We turned back, followed the Gallatin down to the three forks, getting a glimpse of Gallatin City to the west, and struck into the Helena-Diamond City road which led to the ferry across the Missouri below the rapids. Gallatin City was an adobe village of perhaps thirty buildings. Many of the houses were then unoccupied and falling in ruins. Its founders planned to make it the head of navigation by building a railroad around the falls and running smaller boats up from there. The railroad failed to materialize and the project was abandoned.

On our arrival in Helena on the afternoon of the fourth day out, we found the Vigilantes busy with a necktie party in Dry Gulch. The victim – once a Vigilante himself, convicted of robbery – was hanging from the fatal limb when we visited the scene.

The journey to Fort Benton occupied nearly a week. The road was very rough most of the way. From the ferry on Sun river there were no settlers till we struck the Missouri again. Near Sun river, where we joined the Mullan road, we began to hear a dull roaring which increased as we advanced. From freighters we learned that it was the Great Falls. They tell me now that they have harnessed the falls so that they don't roar the way they used to.

Fort Benton was a busy place, at that time the head of navigation. Up to 1853 no steamboats had gone beyond Fort Union, on the Yellowstone; after that the lighter draught boats began running up to the falls during high water.

Several boats were tied up at the landing the afternoon we arrived. One, the Iron City, had pulled out that morning; another had gone up to the falls about forty miles above; and another, the Amelia Poe, had just unloaded. She was a stern-wheeler, like most of the light-draught boats, and was named for the captain's daughter. We engaged passage on this boat and went aboard at once. The horses and wagons were brought on separately. The horses were tied back aft on the lower deck and the wagons were run up on pulleys even with the cabin deck where they were out of the way and at the same time accessible if anything was wanted.

At six we went down to supper. Captain Poe sat at the head of a long table, his men near him, and the rest wherever they chose, family style. The food was abundant and appetizing. Everybody seemed at home. Though a small boat, everything possible was provided for our convenience.

There was a boy of eighteen or nineteen on board who was coming down with typhoid. A companion, a couple of years his senior, was caring for him. They had worked their passage to Fort Benton and intended going on to Helena with some freighting outfit, but decided to return as the boy grew worse. All on board were anxious about the case and no pains were spared for his comfort. Some of the ladies took turns caring for him by day and the men at night.

Fort Benton, Montana, in 1855

We passed Cow island toward evening the first day out. As we approached, a band of black-tail deer bounded up the river bank at our left. Someone on board wantonly shot at them, breaking a leg of their leader.

We tied up for the night about fifteen miles farther on, having accomplished something like 240 miles that day, from six to six. There were no wood yards on the upper Missouri and the deck hands and roustabouts had to go ashore and get what wood was needed for the next day's run before dark. They also brought in cottonwood boughs to supplement the little grain and hay which we were able to get for the horses when we boarded. Boats did not run after nightfall because their insurance would be forfeited.

The second day out, an hour and a half before sundown, we headed for shore, intending to tie up if there was plenty of wood handy. Some of the deckhands landed, but not finding enough they boarded and we swung out again. Just as we were leaving, the swift current forced the stern in shore and the next thing we knew we were impaled on the stub of a tree which projected from shore at an angle of about forty-five degrees. It crashed through the railing and two staterooms, with several feet to spare above. Men were busy at once chopping and clearing away the wreckage, while the boat forged ahead, and we were soon clear. Fortunately no one was in the staterooms and there was no further damage beyond a good scare.

The following afternoon a herd of buffalo came lumbering down the steep bank from the north and started across ahead of us. I had never seen buffalo on one of their migrations. To me it was a thrilling sight as the great shaggy creatures plunged into the swirling waters and struck out boldly for the opposite shore. Captain Poe ordered the boat to slow down and soon we were in the midst of them. Everybody on board that had a gun took a shot at them and each fully believed he had got a buffalo. Five turned over – three cows and two old bulls. They brought in the cows and let the bulls go. I thought it was the best meat I ever tasted.

A couple of days later we thought we saw the smoke from the Iron City, which had left Fort Benton a day ahead of us. Captain Poe wanted to overtake her and we put on steam. After several miles in a fairly straight course, the river made a bend. Here we discovered the Iron City, just heading toward a large lower-river boat near the north shore. Captain Poe recognized her as the Jenny Lewis, loaded with troops. She had come up as far as it was safe for a boat of her draught and was waiting for smaller boats to go on with the troops. Captain Poe did not want to be pressed back. Disregarding their signals, he ordered his boat to pass near the south shore. They fired muskets ahead of him. He kept on, hoping they would use one of the other boats when it came along. Presently, through his glass, he saw them bringing up a six-

FORT UNION

From an original drawing by Charles Bodmer about 1833

pounder. He ordered the Amelia Poe alongside at once.

We spent nearly the whole day transferring to the Jenny Lewis, while the soldiers with their equipment moved aboard the two smaller boats. The Jenny Lewis was a 2,000 ton boat and the other boats were about 250 tons. Everything was different. We were no longer like one big family. The captain and his officers ate at separate tables. The food was poor and there was never enough of it.

When we passed Fort Union, at the mouth of the Yellowstone, we saw several flatboats coming down. They were of various sizes, holding from three or four to twenty or more persons with their goods. Men made a regular business of building flatboats on the upper Yellowstone east of Bozeman pass during the winter and selling them in the spring to parties wishing to go down with the high water. Plank for the boats were "whipped" from logs placed over a pit, one man standing in the pit with his face protected by a cloth, the other above to guide the saw. The width of a boat was about one-third its length; the sides were straight, ends slightly flaring. Protections of lighter plank were set upon the gunwales in case of lurking indians. There was always plenty of canvas to keep out the storms. A man at the bow and another at the stern guided it. Side oars were also used on the larger boats. Sometimes poles served instead.

All boats had to "warp up" over the rapids.

Where water was too swift for a steamboat to proceed further they would head for shore and send men forward with a line. This was fastened to a tree or anything substantial. A small engine then started the "nigger" turning, and the boat steamed ahead, when they would "tie loose" and repeat the process till they were past the swift water.

Near the present Fort Berthold we saw a large village of Sioux and their allies. The plain beyond the high banks was filled with lodges. A steamboat was moored at the foot of a bluff, where a parley seemed to be in progress between the indians and government officials. We drew alongside a few minutes to watch the proceedings. Chiefs in full feather and officers were gathered about a large table and clerks were busy taking down statements. Negotiations were under way designating the Missouri as the eastern boundary of the Sioux territory. Preliminary arrangements were begun the fall before on Sully's visit. This meeting was another step in the boundary settlement.

Our sick boy grew steadily worse. There was no physician aboard, but medicines were obtained from forts along the way. His pal rarely left him for long.

The day we reached Fort Rice a storm was gathering. We tied up at the landing in the late afternoon. Two bow-lines and a stern-line were thrown out and made fast, one by an anchor buried in the earth, the others to trees. At midnight after my turn beside the sick bed, the other boy relieved me and I rolled up in my blankets on the boiler deck within easy reach if I was needed.

My slumbers were cut short by a terrific crash of thunder as the storm broke in all its fury. On the cabin deck confusion reigned. People were running about in a frenzy of fright. There were shouts, cries, groans, curses, and frantic attempts to bring order out of the turmoil. The boat lurched, snapping the lines as though they were packthread, and the next moment we were adrift.

Firemen rushed down in their night clothes and raked the coals together under the boilers, throwing on grease, pieces of bacon, light wood – anything to start a quick fire. Above the din came sounds of breaking timbers as we drifted against the rocky shore wall.

I ran back aft, returned with a piece of plank, and waited. Presently we were caught by the current and carried toward the south shore. After endless minutes the wheels began to turn. Suddenly we slid up on a sandbar and there we stuck. Daylight showed that we had run down a couple of miles before we stranded. Had there been but one cable instead of three, we might have turned over at the first blast; and without a friendly sandbar to catch us there is no knowing what new perils lay in wait. Which goes to show that if a man is destined to hang he won't drown.

It took us till ten o'clock that forenoon to pull off from the bar. After steaming back to the landing we tied up for the rest of the day.

Watchers beside the sick-bed realized that the lad who had fared forth so blithely only a few short weeks before was face to face with the Big Adventure. In the small hours of the morning he "slipit awa." The body was taken to the fort and prepared for burial. Seasoned veterans of the wilds and home folks alike were drawn together by a common bond as we left the little cemetery on the hill and resumed our journey.

We had passed successively through regions of deep rich soil, through great stretches of yellow clay, through badlands with their weird formations; now we were entering the upper edge of the Sand hills, where the current was as shifting as the transient sandbars. The scenery whizzed by at the rate of twenty miles an hour on the average. The only signs of life were the military posts and the passing steamboats.

Dissatisfaction over the scarcity of food was growing daily. There was always a grand rush for the first table where they could be reasonably sure of enough to eat. When the next relay came in they cleaned things up pretty well. The third tableful got what was left – and usually there wasn't anything left.

Passengers gathered for a free discussion of the situation. People had paid their fare, it was urged, and were entitled to food sufficient for their needs. Several posts had been passed, and no attempt made to obtain provisions. At the close of the meeting volunteers offered to go to the captain, talk things over with him, and ask him to find a remedy.

The captain received the committee and very readily promised relief. There was general rejoicing at the prospect of enough to eat, but it was short-lived. Another post was passed and no effort made to get supplies. Matters grew worse, if possible. Finally another meeting was held – an indignation meeting. There were mountain men, freighters, miners, all armed and ready for action. Including those from the Amelia Poe and Iron City, between eighty and a hundred men could be counted on. Word was sent to the captain that if the food shortage was not relieved at once, the passengers would take charge of the boat and handle the situation.

Right then and there the captain got busy. At the smaller posts and at Fort Randall all available supplies were purchased. We tied up early at Niobrara and scoured the country till midnight for butter, eggs, meat, everything in the line of eatables. No further complaint was heard about lack of food.

At the end of thirteen days, or ten days' running time, we landed at Sioux City and set out at once for Wisconsin. We spent the Fourth with the Francis family, on East Okaboja, and participated in a charivari in honor of an aunt of the Francis children, who had taken a husband the day before our arrival. Tom and I had a good boat ride on the lake.

A few days later we reached La Crosse. I had driven an ox-team across the Plains 1700 miles to Gallatin valley, returned by boat down the Missouri 2100 miles, with a good 600 miles more across country with horses to complete the circle – in all about 4500 miles. I had spent two of the most interesting years of my life "Out Where the West Begins." And now it was time to go home and see my mother.

The lure of the old Mississippi and the lumber camps was too strong. After visiting my mother, who was widowed by the war, I made my plans anew; and the first snowfall found me running an edging saw in North La Crosse. Thereafter, until I was of age, I sorted logs each summer at Halfway Point, just above North La Crosse and spent the winters hunting and trapping down the river as far as Hale's Point, Tennessee.

Following Horace Greeley's injunction, I then homesteaded in Nebraska, freighted on the Pierre trail, traded with indians and ranchers in the Dakotas and Montana, and finally settled with my family in northern Wyoming.

The Ridgleys returned to Gallatin valley the next spring, where they lived prosperously until Mr. Ridgley's death in December, 1870. He lies buried in the old cemetery between his old neighbors, J. M. Bozeman and Nelson Story. Mrs. Ridgley returned to her home in Wisconsin where she lived many years. I visited her in 1890, and she said, "Jerome, I want to cook one more meal for you." She was then in her eighties.

Near my home in the shadow of the Big Horns three great roads intersect: the Bozeman trail, the Burlington railroad and the Custer battlefield highway. Over the point of intersection a few days ago we could see an airplane winging its way along the proposed air-mail route between Cheyenne and Great Falls.

Some one asked me which way I had rather travel, by ox-team or airplane. I did not need to ponder the question. I'd rather chance the oxen.

Index

Index